D0464075

Is God Deaf?

Is God Deaf?

A Meditation on Prayer

PIERRE WOLFF

COWLEY PUBLICATIONS
Cambridge, Massachusetts

Published in the United States of America by Cowley Publications, a
division of the Society of St. John the Evangelist. No portion of this
book may be reproduced, stored in or introduced into a retrieval system, or transmitted, in any form or by any means—including photo-
copying—without the prior written permission of Cowley
Publications, except in the case of brief quotations embodied in criti-
cal articles and reviews.

International Standard Book Number: 1-56101-030-8
Library of Congress Number: 84-070037

Library of Congress Cataloging-in-Publication Data
Wolff, Pierre, 1929-
Is God deaf? : a meditation on prayer / Pierre Wolff.
p. cm.
Revised Edition. Originally published: New Jersey : Arena Lettres,
c1984.
ISBN 1-56101-030-8 (alk. paper)
1. Prayer—Christianity. I. Title.
BV215.W62 1991
248.3'2-dc20   90-25879

This book is printed on acid-free paper and was produced in the
United States of America.

Cover illustration by Susan Mangam

Cowley Publications
28 Temple Place
Boston, Massachusetts 02111

Silently,
with Mary,
who conceived, bore, and delivered
the Word of the Father in our flesh;
who listened to the boy's cries
from the first to the last,
as the Father did,
lovingly.

Thank you to all the people who have revealed to me what is summarized in this book: their "silence" has been so powerful!

Thank you, Marie-Therese, for making my words so beautiful in your language.

TABLE OF CONTENTS

INTRODUCTION

HARD QUESTIONS TO ANSWER

The desire to write this book was born through questions about prayer that I have heard for years.

The most common and the simplest one has been, "What is prayer life?" I have become less and less at ease in answering this question, for the reality lived and revealed to me by people goes beyond the explanations. How many times, for example, have I heard retreatants trying to describe a spiritual experience and finally giving up their attempt, saying, "I cannot find the right words to express what I have felt." Something deep always seems to escape explanation.

Another kind of assertion has also struck me very often: "I am sorry, but I pray only ten minutes a day." The first person who admitted this to me, twenty years ago, was an engineer dedicated to his family, his business and his duties as a citizen. I still hear myself wondering, "Is he praying ten minutes a day, or twenty-four hours a day?" I ask myself if we do not sometimes live with a very narrow definition of prayer.

Still another kind of question came up with a friend of mine when she tried to understand how it was possible to accomplish the desire of Paul, "Pray unceasingly" (1 Thessalonians 5:17). If Paul invites us to this so forcefully, we cannot avoid seeking an answer—but an answer for every Christian, not only for monks.

Finally, those who deal with suffering persons in convalescent homes or mental institutions, in prisons or in slums, live constantly with the question, "Is it possible to pray in such a terrible situation? What kind of prayer life is possible here?" The question is justified; what kind of prayer can exist in a crushed and broken heart, in a body barely alive?

But I have also been asked other questions about prayer. I have met people who seem to pray very easily, *too* easily. They told me they had a lasting, "nice" feeling of God's presence and gave me descriptions of their prayer life that I often found too simplistic. Because I have had the opportunity to verify—in retreats, for instance—that some of these persons considered ambiguous spiritual behavior or devotions as genuine prayer life, I felt that they were carefully cultivating a centeredness in self that gave little space for the Lord's word within themselves.

So what can we say about prayer?

"PRAY UNCEASINGLY"

First, a fact: every time I talked with people about their prayer life, I perceived in them a kind of certainty.

Behind the worries of those who thought that they were not praying enough, and behind the too-immediate assurance of those who were satisfied with their prayer, there was a feeling that a relationship between themselves and God had always been present. We never could elucidate how this feeling could remain so strong or how it could be justified, but this difficulty is not surprising.

Like other questions about the spiritual life, those concerning prayer confront us with the impossible task of explaining the relationship between a human being and God. If we believed that we could accomplish such an undertaking, we would be claiming that we could define God and a human being, and what can happen between them. What presumption this would be! Humbly we must admit that we can only come close to some ideas of these mysteries.

But now I think that the vague feeling of people I have met may become a certainty: whether with ease or not, *we pray unceasingly.* We all do, in all kinds of situations, but probably not in the way we think. The purpose of this book is to try to demonstrate this, in order to give hope to those who think they do not pray, and to help those who pray too superficially to deepen their prayer life.

ORDINARY TEACHING ABOUT PRAYER

But why not simply go back to the usual teaching about prayer to find the answers to these questions? No doubt, we could; but we must be conscious of a defect found almost everywhere. Books which treat the subject of prayer deal more or less with the following topics: general thoughts about prayer; methods of prayer, such as meditation with the intellect; contemplation with the imagination; how to use the body while praying; the prayer of silence. Some chapters take up prayer in or with the Scriptures, and the prayer of Jesus himself as a model. Sometimes we find an explanation of the various stages of prayer life, leading from externalized articulation to a silent internal attitude before the Lord.

The starting point is usually a formal method of praying. Prayer is seen as *an action we have to do*. We have to say some words; we have to find some thoughts in our mind; we have to picture some images within ourselves; we have to create a void in our depths; we have to look for a center. *We always have to do something in order to be praying.* There is so much insistence on the practice of the means described that we soon come up against a problem: if we cannot follow the proposed method for twenty-four hours a day (and we cannot), then we must say, "I cannot pray unceasingly," or, like the engineer previously quoted, "I pray only a few minutes a day." This leads us to despair, or to another method we think will be more effective, for we think that the greater part of our life is "prayerless."

So to solve this problem, the authors (and I with them) explain that all our actions can become prayers. They tell us, for instance, to offer the day to the Lord in the morning, or to offer the present moment at any time, and the twenty-four hours of the day will be transformed into prayer. This is true; but what if we forget the morning offering, if we are too distracted during the day? After all, it is probably better for a bus driver to concentrate on the road than to be consciously offering anything to anyone. At least it is safer for the people on the bus!

Then the authors might say that because we are baptized, the whole of our life is already offered and consecrated to the Lord, the whole of our life is a prayer. True; but should we not live this consecration more consciously? Of course we should; but how? There is only one way: to relate consciously to the gift of our baptismal life as frequently as possible during the day. But this brings us back to the impossibility of consciously praying for twenty-four consecutive hours. So, in the ordinary teaching about prayer something is missing that could help us to fulfill the wish of Paul, "Pray unceasingly."

Some people tell us that they are aware of the Lord all day long. What do they mean? Some of them live a style of life which allows them to have this experience; for instance, religious who live in a specific environment that fosters the conditions for it. The best model for this is the life of monks whose schedule is organized to favor the spiritual life. It is quite difficult to imagine this for lay people who work in factories or offices, yet Paul's advice is for everyone!

In some cases, we have reservations about people who claim to be constantly aware of God's presence. Sometimes they seem to be so far removed from the real world that we are skeptical about the truth of their so-called spiritual experience. How could God, who created us and the world, desire a prayer that makes us escape from the very place in which he wants us to live and work? So if prayer were only what we have described above, it would be really difficult for *everyone* to fulfill the command of Paul.

OBSTACLES

If prayer places us and maintains us outside of the world, where are we then? What kind of communion are we living with our brothers and sisters? If there is prayer only when words are pronounced, how miserable are those who cannot speak fluently and easily, those who are shy and quiet, those who cannot be outspoken, articulate and exuberant, those who are imprisoned in silence by suffering. If there is prayer only when thoughts or images are present, unhappy are those who are not thinkers or artists, those whose education has never developed such gifts, those who cannot read or write, those whose heads are tortured by suffering. If there is prayer only when an inner void has been created, unfortunate are those who are preoccupied with grave questions, necessary worries, and vital problems. If there is prayer only when it is easy to pray, what about those who have to face years of interior dryness? If there is prayer only when we are conscious of ourselves, what happens when we are asleep; when we undergo surgery under anesthesia; or when a coma anticipates the sleep of death? If there is prayer only when we are ourselves, what about those who are mentally disturbed or insane?

If we do not go beyond the usual teaching about prayer, we are helpless before these situations. We must find an explanation of prayer that deals with these problems, for it would be unthinkable to accept a prayer life that removes people from reality, or that excludes people from the possibility of a genuine life of prayer. We are convinced that prayer keeps us *in* life, and that every kind of life has room for prayer.

But the worst obstacle is not mentioned in the above list. If we believe that there is prayer only when something is *done* by us, what kind of God do we suggest?

In fact, *a God who is deaf.*

He is deaf indeed if we always have to make noise—words, thoughts, images—to get him to pay attention, to force him to be aware of us. He is deaf if we have to empty ourselves of all the things dwelling within us, as if they were obstacles to his hearing us. And when praying is *too* easy, when we experience a river of words, thoughts and images, when we still *do* a lot by ourselves, we try to make him deaf.

We might say that the more we *do* in our prayer life, the more we confess, perhaps, a God who is or is made deaf. And so Elijah's mockery of the prophets of Baal is aimed at us when he says, "Call louder, for he is a god. It may be that he is deep in thought, or engaged, or on a journey; or he may have gone to sleep and must be woken up" (1 Kings 18:27). Or maybe the words of Jesus are meant for us: "Do not rattle on like the pagans" (Matthew 6:8).

Just as we know that we do pray unceasingly without being able to explain it, we know that our God cannot be deaf. We must explain how and why this is so. It is bad enough to meet people who act as though they are deaf when we speak to them; if our God were like this, it would be terrible for us. And it would also be terrible if God could be made deaf. Perhaps because we do not always hear others, we think God is also deaf; perhaps because others do not always listen to us, we think God is deaf as well—especially when we are the lowliest ones of the world, handicapped, mentally disturbed, terminally ill, or too poor and uneducated for sophisticated methods of praying.

We must understand prayer life in such a way that we will have the answers to our questions and the assurance that

- everyone prays;

- and everyone prays unceasingly.

In this way the feeling of always being in touch with God will become clear. And above all, people who were born silent under the weight of mystery, who grew silent under the pressure of suffering, who die silent under the burden of a terrible fate without ever having had the right to express themselves, will not be excluded from the framework of prayer life. If we could not find a life of prayer in a mentally ill person, for instance, our God would really be deaf. But as soon as we accept the fact that everyone has a heart, including God, we can admit that prayer is possible for all.

We shall also see how we try to make God deaf at times. Maybe we want him to be deaf because we do not want to hear with him what he hears, because we are afraid to listen with him to all the cries that come to him.

So we have defined the two main parts of this book in terms of two types of deafness: God's and ours. Words are clumsy when they try to describe relations between us and God. Therefore if this book still uses words, they will serve to call us into silence. In fact, the subject is really silence.

THE BOY'S CRY

SOMETHING IS PRESENT BEYOND...

Let us recall some experiences we have all known either personally or through others. They will provide the focus for the first part of our reflection.

What did they say? Could we hear?

- We have all seen, at least on television, crowds burying their dead after a riot. The people of Lebanon, Chile, Iran, Vietnam, Cambodia and other countries are still in our memories, as are the funerals of John F. Kennedy, Martin Luther King, Nasser, Boumedienne, Chou en Lai. What were the crowds really saying behind their silence or their shouts?

- We remember the faces of those men and women of the Sahel, Uganda and Cambodia; those refugees from South Vietnam with their babies dying of starvation or disease in their arms. They were seemingly as impassive as blocks of marble. But what could we read in their eyes?

11

- Sharon's dog is dead. She runs to her mother in tears. The mother understands. What do we hear?

- The victims have been starving for days. The rescue team arrives. Food, blankets, and medicine are immediately distributed from their trucks. Each victim receives provision. As they leave their eyes gaze upon the givers. What are they saying?

- An announcement is made to the workers: many of them will soon be unemployed. They leave the factory in silence. As they pass the employer's office, they wordlessly look through the window. Can we hear a cry?

But then, on the other hand:

- I can still see Jimmy near the Christmas tree when he was six years old. He had been longing for a promised toy, a car with pedals. When it came out of its box, shiny red, he clapped his hands and stamped his feet. He was speechless, but what did he tell us?

- Dennis is playing baseball wearing his new T-shirt. On it is written, "Behind this T-shirt is one terrific kid." He hits nine home runs in a row, so sure is he of the shirt's magic. What does his radiant face say to us?

- Thousands of people are at the game between the two best teams in the country. Suddenly a goal! Like a single person we all stand up, shouting. Beyond our shouts, what are we saying?

- They told me that after making love they usually remain in each other's arms for a long time, silently. Silently?

- After receiving the Body of Christ, Dominique, a little blonde girl of eight, rested her head on her arms for a long time. She was silent, but did she really say nothing?

- They lost their first baby. Now the second is born. The father and mother look at each other. There are no words, only tears in their eyes and on their cheeks. Can we hear what they are saying to each other?

A message difficult to put into words

We understand what emerges from these examples. Even though we do not hear any clear expression with our ears, something is "said" A message, happy or sad, comes through in each of those situations. We might say that the crowds mourning their dead were sorrowful, that the people of Cambodia were crushed, that Jimmy was happy. Would we be sure we were right?

We cannot prove the truth of our suppositions. Only through talking with the people concerned would we be able to verify the truth of our interpretations. Some of them would probably express feelings that more or less matched our own impressions, but many of them would undoubtedly be unable to explain clearly what they felt and why. It is always difficult to express feelings that are too deep and too intense for words. We all know what it is like to be unable to find the words we want to say when a feeling is inexpressible. The overflow of happiness or sadness is such that we cannot find a way to articulate it.

THERE IS TOO MUCH BEHIND ANY WORD

- "When they put my twenty-one year old sister in the casket," she told me, "I just broke down in tears."

- As we drove home after giving our first retreat in prison, we were so deeply moved by what we had seen and heard that we cried. One of us could only repeat over and over, "I am speechless."

- After we had heard Leonard Bernstein conduct Mahler's Ninth Symphony, we could not express in words what we felt. My friend drove in silence; I hammered my knee with my fist. Something within us had been powerfully touched.

In these instances, without a doubt a message was present. It was so intensely happy or unhappy that it could not be put into words.

An overflow

When we have such strong feelings, there is obviously no void within us. The forceful message born in our depths is conveyed more or less accurately. Observers see that something important has happened to us, that we are not empty but too full. Whether or not they guess the nature of our experience, our outward behavior betrays its depth. Sometimes the power overflowing from us is so strong that they too are caught up in it and are similarly impressed, unable like us to express it in words. The lack of words reveals the excess of our emotion. And our usual ability or inability to express ourselves has nothing to do with it.

- When we arrived at the scene of a terrible accident on the highway, five bodies were already strewn about on the road. In one car the driver was wedged behind the wheel with his legs crushed. As his wife lay dying beside him, he repeated over and over. "Why did he drive into me?" Many of us were so upset by such a drama that we could not sleep for several nights. We could never adequately express the feelings that overflowed at this scene of horror.

• The audience stood after the Hallelujah Chorus of Handel's *Messiah*. After a brief silence, some started to applaud. Then the contagion seized everyone, and the entire audience exploded in whistling, clapping and shouting.

• As we stood by the ocean, we chatted quietly. One after another we stopped talking while the sunset began to caress the golden sand. It was so magnificent that we were engulfed in deep silence. Someone occasionally murmured, "This is too much..."

A void? Certainly not. The message conveyed by means other than words was too powerful, too contagious, to allow anyone to feel emptiness within. Such an overwhelming event cannot be treated as insignificant; it often marks our lives. It always reminds me of the verse in the Book of Revelation: "There was a silence in heaven for what seemed half an hour" (8: 1).

Is this indefinable but precious message lost?

As a matter of fact, we can generally say something about what we have felt. But since the emotions are so strong, we can usually describe them only in a negative **way.** If people try to help us identify our feeling, we can immediately sense the wrongness of an interpretation and unhesitatingly say, "No, that is not it." But we are not able to be specific in a positive way. If by ourselves or with the help of others we approach a description, we always feel that something escapes us.

When our mind cannot find the right words, our body betrays us. It shows clearly that something happened or is happening inside. So great is the overflow of our feelings that they inevitably manifest themselves through body language.

- In the waiting room a friend of mine waits to hear the result of her husband's serious operation. She constantly moves her feet, strums on the desk with her fingers, and smokes one cigarette after another.

- In the unforgettable face and body of an old woman in Appalachia are inscribed both the misery of three generations on welfare and the peace acquired through deep faith.

- During a contest we saw teams of swimmers "dancing" a graceful ballet. The postures of the young bodies were a beautiful hymn to life.

• On May 8, 1945, the dances in the streets of my nation were themselves a hymn to peace and freedom.

The body betrays us when something is happening deep inside us. Even if nothing appears exteriorly, something is at work within. Strong emotions make us hot or cold, hungry or thirsty, for instance. Scars and wrinkles, healthy muscles, are signs unveiling a message. Something is said in some way, like a song, a prayer.

When we see body language, we cannot interpret in words the message we get from someone else. That is why we make mistakes when we try to understand or put into words the behavior of others. He looks cold, but he is really shy. She seems indifferent, but she is really trying to keep control of herself He appears strong and calm, but he is protecting himself against our feelings, or his own. We can remember our own experiences—how often we have misunderstood or been misunderstood.

Could we ever imagine that all of this would be lost just because it was impossible to express it in a comprehensible way? Could we believe that all those precious feelings would be wasted because they lacked conscious expression? Wordless hope, inarticulate hate, silent supplication, inexpressible joy, speechless admiration: are these not priceless? We know too well their impact on our lives, the price we have paid for them, to think that no one could hear or understand them. Maybe *we* are often deaf...but is there someone close enough to us to know what our being expresses, to understand our cries as prayers?

THE LORD HEARS

Our mistakes

We do not always have the answer to the question, "Is there someone who hears our unconscious expressions?" That may be because we look at prayer only from our own point of view: what *we* are aware of, what *we* do and feel.

A first mistake consists in thinking that there can be prayer only when we are conscious that we pray—as if our being were mute when our tongue is. Our examples have clearly shown that overflowing life beneath the surface cannot be ignored or excluded from prayer. It is part of our prayer, but how?

A second mistake is to forget that the Lord is not limited by anything. He is God and not a human being.

The third mistake is the most serious. In our conception of prayer we somehow forget the One who is its object and make ourselves the center of the action. Since prayer is communication, we cannot put aside the other partner. The common understanding of prayer overemphasizes what *we* do, as if our partner were totally passive. A transmitter cannot function without a receiver; when the receiver is not working, the transmitter is useless. Prayer has to be centered on the Lord; therefore, we must look at it from his side too.

* They have lost their baby. We are with them in silence. Could our silence be lost to God?

* During the battle we took some prisoners. Wives and children stared at us as we dragged away their husbands and fathers. Was their message ignored by God?

* Behind the house, our patrol suddenly came upon a child of six or seven. As soon as the child saw the soldiers, he raised his hands above his head. We were shocked that one so young already knew the meaning of "Hands up!" Can we imagine God indifferent?

"The boy's cry"
If our notion of God is correct and if we believe in him, it is impossible to think that he has the same limitations, the same deafness, as we do. Our heart would rebel against a God who ignored our situation. We would say with the Psalmist, "Shall he who shaped the ear not hear?" (Psalm 94:9). We may hear or not hear, others may or may not perceive our fear or joy...but Someone hears.

When the depth of a human being cries out, God hears it.

We find this certainty in the first personal prayer of the Bible. In Genesis, Abraham is forced by his wife Sarah to drive out Hagar, his concubine, and his first son, Ishmael.

As Hagar roamed aimlessly in the wilderness of Beersheba, the water in the skin was used up. So she put the child down under a shrub and then went and sat down opposite him, about a bowshot away; for she said to herself, "Let me not watch the child die." As she sat opposite him, he began to cry. God heard the boy's cry, and God's messenger called to Hagar from heaven, "What is the matter, Hagar? Do not be afraid; God has heard the boy's cry in this plight of his." (Genesis 21:14b-17)

Where could we find something more unconscious, more difficult to understand, than a child's cry? A cry from the depths. And the Scriptures tell us that God heard "the boy's cry."

God hears us

God hears the cries of all human beings. He hears the cries of starving people as well as the cry of a child thrilled with a Christmas gift. Therefore, since the Lord hears what we express not with our lips but within our hearts, an unfailing communication is established between him and us. Even when we cover up the inner message with too many words, thoughts and images, *he* hears the deepest cries of our being. It does not matter if we are conscious of the message sent out by our "transmitter." The "receiver" who is God is always tuned to our frequency—to the deepest one that is never turned off for him.

This kind of communication, in which our message reaches God, may be called prayer. This is so even when we are unconscious of our message or when we try to cover it up.

Therefore, *we always pray; everyone always prays.* For our being always cries out something, and God always hears it.

I am sure that those who are schizophrenic or autistic have within themselves something to express. Experts say that autistic children stop walking and start to swing their bodies in places frequented by others, but never in isolated places where people never pass by. Is this not already "communication" with others? Even if we do not understand the meaning of signs like that, Someone does. A movie about an autistic boy shows him fascinated in the contemplation of a creek. If this is a mystery for us, it is not for the Lord. No heart is so dead that it cannot send a message, and God always hears it. Studies of persons in a coma lead us to think that some communication with them may exist for us. How much more for the Lord who hears the heart that is still alive.

With the same logic and faith, I am sure that God also hears the cries dwelling in the hearts of unbelievers. Such people, of course, have no desire or reason to pray to him; but could we picture the Lord indifferent to them, just because they have no religious faith? As human beings they share the same joys and sorrows as believers. So God hears them too.

This is why we may say with certainty that *everyone prays: because God hears everyone cry.*

When we look at it from God's point of view, our being always prays because God always hears "the boy's cry" within us.

- It is consoling for the parents of a handicapped child to know that their son is heard and understood by the Lord, even though not by them.

- It gives strength to those who are powerless before dying people, "lost" cases in prison, to know that God is not deaf, that he hears the depths of such people better than we can when we have done our best.

- It helps one experiencing a nervous breakdown and undergoing psychotherapy, unable to communicate, and feeling misunderstood, to know that Someone, God himself, is listening.

• Some people deal with beings so deformed and disturbed, so abnormal, that we sometimes hesitate to call them human: for example, "The Elephant Man." The grace of faith enables us to believe that God listens to them, that they are his sons and daughters.

A listening God

No one hears us unless he or she is ready to hear us, unless he or she is already listening. Authentic hearing presupposes a disposition to listen. I believe that the Lord hears us because *he is listening to us.*

This means that his attention is focused on us before (if we may use this word about God) a cry is uttered. It implies that God is attentive to us and our situations, to our intimate feelings and reactions. We can picture him as our creator, aware of us and of our inner life with nothing able to escape him. If God should forget or ignore us for even a millionth of a second, we would immediately disappear into nothingness; we are sustained in existence precisely because he is always attentive to us. Our lives depend totally on his attention. This God who is so interested in our existence must be seen as always listening to us. As a matter of fact, I am only describing the God of Exodus, who says in chapters 3 and 6:

I have witnessed the affliction of my people in Egypt and have heard their cry of complaint against their slave drivers, so I know well what they are suffering. And now that I have heard the groaning of the Israelites, whom the Egyptians are treating as slaves, I am mindful of my covenant.

This listening God is also the one celebrated in Psalm 139:

O Lord, you have probed me and you know me; You know when I sit and when I stand; You understand my thoughts from afar...Even before a word is on my tongue, Behold, 0 Lord, you know the whole of it.

A loving God
The fact that God not only hears us but listens to us makes a difference. If I hear you, it means that you are the one who starts the communication, and that I receive your message only after you have expressed yourself. Hearing gives priority of action to the one who expresses himself or herself. But when I listen to you, I am the one who begins the interchange. Before you say anything, I am ready to hear you, already focused on you and your plight, already open to what you are going to express. Such an attitude signifies care, attention, concern and interest on my part before you say anything. Is this not love?

- She was asleep in bed. We knew that it was surely the last time we would see her alive. We helped her to waken peacefully. It was a long time before we succeeded. But when she opened her eyes and smiled, she could see the love in our gaze, already demonstrated through our patient gentleness. A listening God is a loving God. A God who loves us cannot be deaf; and a God who is not deaf is a loving God.

ALWAYS PREGNANT WITH A CRY

Thus we pray unceasingly because the Lord is always listening to us. But we have also qualified our prayer as unceasing because we said that our being is always crying out. Is it certain that we are always pregnant with a cry?

Our cries

Everyone will agree that, in the examples we have given, the conception, bearing and delivery of a human cry took place in people's hearts through a specific happening. Crushed or enlivened, those men and women went through difficult moments or enjoyed exciting ones, and thus experienced the creation and growth of a cry. Every time we live a fundamental human situation, we go through the same thing. A cry is conceived, carried, and developed within us. Sometimes it is born and manifested exteriorly;

even when it is not, it is always inside, though hidden. It is a cry of hatred or anger when we are frustrated; a cry of anguish or uncertainty when the future is threatening; a cry of fear or panic when we are in danger; a cry of suffering or sorrow when we are hurt. It is a cry of exultation or joy when we are happy; a cry of praise or delight when we are caught up in admiration; a cry of plenitude or love when we are fulfilled. And there are so many other cries that express all the impulses of our body, mind and heart when the depth of our being is touched. Arthur Janov's theory of the "primal scream" may be relevant to what we are saying here; how many cries we have repressed in our lives? How many cries would have escaped since we were born if we had been free enough to let them come out? How many repressed cries since that first cry, the one that meant we were alive?

The ordinary cry of life

The examples we have quoted were all rare occurrences, but they illustrated the diverse and numerous facets of one unique cry: the cry of life. All the events described were assaults and aggressions against life, or revelations and ecstasies magnifying life. These particular situations illustrate the extremes of the dying or developing

of the cry of common daily life. Even when nothing uncommon happens, life is still a cry—the
most enduring and astounding one. Life is a
struggle carried on every day. It presupposes a lasting energy that keeps us going, a
continuing cry of our being. Life is a confronta-
tion with every day, either painful or joyful. A
simple example: how often do we feel tired and
lazy on Monday morning when our alarm clock
tries to wake us up? We groan, and we need a
great deal of energy to get up, to go to work.
When we are eager to stay in bed longer every
morning, it is usually because we would like to
escape the daily battle. At other times we jump
out of bed full of life, happy to greet a new day,
eager to do what we have to do. The jump is like a
cry before a contest we wish to win. To be and to
live is a challenge, a decision we either face with
energy or refuse with resignation. A cry of life
that wants to succeed, or a cry of life that chooses
to die. The desire to live is such an important cry
that it is a real sign of hope when it is perceived in
persons tempted to suicide or stricken with grave
illness. When it disappears, death is present even
before the person has departed physically. Some
people die before passing away. When the body
continues to live on until physical death, perhaps
it is refusing the mind's resignation, or awaiting
in its members the end already accepted by the
spirit.

Our whole life is circumscribed within two cries: the first and the last breath, the cry of birth and of death. But breathing or gasping for breath, we are heard by God. We are always pregnant with a cry, a desire he listens to.

A desire

All our cries express a longing, a desire seeking fulfillment or temporarily fulfilled. It may be the desire for peace, justice, nourishment, victory, a job, a gift, rescue. It may also be desire for a person: the return of intimacy with a lover, the birth of a child, communion with friends, the presence of God.

Desire lasts as long as life does. Desire is our unceasing prayer, if we believe St. Augustine's words about Psalm 38:10: "O Lord, all my desire is before you, from you my groaning is not hid":

> For not before men, who cannot see the heart, but before you is my every desire. Let your desire be before him, so that the Father who sees in secret may reward you. For your very desire is your prayer. And if your desire is continuous, so is your prayer.
>
> Not for nothing did the Apostle say "Pray constantly" (1 Thessalonians 5:17). Surely we do not kneel, prostrate the body or lift up our hands constantly, so that he says, "Pray without ceasing?" If this is the way we say that we pray, I think we cannot do so constantly. There is another interior constant prayer, which is desire. Whatever else you may do, if you desire that Sabbath, you do not stop praying. If you do not wish to stop

praying, then do not stop desiring. As your desire is continuous, continuous is your voice. You will be mute if you cease to love...Thus we keep silence with our mouth so that we can cry aloud with our heart.

Augustine said also in a sermon on Psalm 85:

For he who desires sings with his heart, even though his tongue is silent. He who does not desire, however, let him beat the ears of men with his cry as much as he likes; he is mute to God.

And finally, he says of Psalm 102:2:

God has ears; he has also a heart...your inmost being is never lacking to him who hears.

I have only extended the notion of desire (that concerns the Sabbath in some of Augustine's comments) to the whole of our life, with its ordinary and extraordinary cries. We cry out for justice or restitution, for assurance or security. We cry out through thanks or praise, loving or merely living. We cry out to human beings for and through these things. And beyond them, we cry out to God. Our faith answers with the Psalmist:

The poor call out. God listens to them (34:7).

You have granted him his heart's desire; you refused not the wish of his lips (21:3).

The desire of the afflicted you hear, 0 Lord (10: 17).

HIS OWN WORD MADE FLESH

If we believe in the God of the Bible, we cannot say anything other than what we have already said. The Lord who "blew into the nostrils" of Adam the "breath of life" (Genesis 2:7), his own Spirit, hears our breathing. He listens to the outpouring of all the cries, conscious or not, that we have described. But the revelation of the New Testament gives us deeper reasons for believing that God is not deaf, that he is always aware of the cry we carry within us, for the New Testament tells us that Jesus was the Son of God.

God's Word made our own

As Christians we believe that the Word of God, the second Person of the Trinity, willed to become one of us. In his Incarnation he took on our flesh and became a human being, Jesus. For thirty-three years the Word uttered by God eternally was a human word. For the length of a human lifetime, the Son spoke with the Father in a human manner. God's Word was *our* word. The everlasting intimate dialogue of the two Persons through the Spirit became in our time and space a human-divine conversation. Human lips, tongue and heart became the divine partner of the Father in heaven. The mysterious and inexpressible intercourse that takes place eternally between the Father and his perfect image and likeness was carried on in human flesh. Can we imagine that such total communion was interrupted when Jesus slept or sounded the depths of death, that the Father stopped hearing and listening to his beloved Son for a while? No; nothing could or can suspend the exchange of love between Father and Son.

Our word made God's

For thirty-three years, all human cries were the Son's; for we believe that Jesus did not refuse to feel what we feel. To think otherwise would be contrary to his "being born in the likeness of men" (Philippians 2:7). He shared everything which is ours, from the joy of a wedding to the sorrow of death (John 2-11:35); from fatigue and rejoicing (John 4:6; Luke 10: 2 1) to loneliness and agony (Matthew 26) and death (Philippians 2:8). "It was our infirmities he bore, our sufferings he endured," says Matthew (8:17). Even though as the man without sin he never allowed the evil touch of our selfishness to distort his feelings and actions, he knew all our cries, including our "Why?" to God (Mark 15:34). For thirty-three years the depth of a human being cried out lovingly to the Father, perfectly in tune with him, and was always lovingly heard. From the baby's cry in the manger of Bethlehem to the dying man's last gasp on the cross in Jerusalem, God the

Father always listened to his "boy's cry." He did it so perfectly and with such love that Jesus could even say *beforehand*, "Father, I thank you for having heard me. I know that you always hear me" (John 11: 41-42).

We might say that the Father understands our cries more clearly because for a while they were his own Son's. It is almost as if the Father "learned" through his Son our human expressions. God learned what it was like to be a human being. Borrowing our language, the Son made our cries his own, and now God listens to our cry because our human language is his Son's forever.

We might sum this up with some verses of Mary's lullaby to Jesus, by a French poet, Marie Noel.

> O my God, you had no mouth
> To talk to those who were lost here below.
> Your milky mouth turned toward my breast, O my son,
> it is I who have given it to you.
>
> O my God, you had no hand
> To heal with your touch their poor tired bodies.
> Your hand, an unopened bud, a rose not yet unfolded,
> my son, it is I who have given it to you.
>
> O my God, you had no flesh
> To break bread with them.
> Your flesh fashioned from my springtime,
> O my son, it is I who have given it to you.
>
> O my God, you had no death
> To save the world with...
> Your death on a dark, forsaken evening,
> 0 my little one, it is I who have given it to you.

Temples of the Spirit

Not only is God attentive to us because we are his creatures, not only does he hear us because his own Son was one of us, but now the Father listens to us because Jesus has given us his Spirit. As God breathed his Spirit into the flesh of the first human being, Jesus breathed his Spirit into his disciples and sent the Spirit to the Church in the name of the Father (John 20:22; Acts 2). We believe that we have received the Spirit of the Risen One. Christ guarantees this presence of the Spirit when he says to his disciples, "You can recognize him because he remains with you and will be with you" (John 14:17). Through the Spirit within us, the words of Jesus are ours, and our words are his (John 16:13-15). Paul says the same thing when he writes to the Romans, "The Word is near you, already on your lips and in your heart" (Romans 10:8). Through our cries, then, the Father hears Someone—his own Word breathed forth by the Spirit in the depth of our being.

This expression dwells so profoundly within our hearts that it cannot always be perceived by us; but according to our faith and "in a manner known only to God," it is present and praying in every human being. "We do not know how to pray as we ought; but the Spirit himself makes intercession for us with groanings that cannot be expressed in speech," as Paul himself points out (Romans 8:26). The mystery of our deepest cries is revealed: it is a Person, the Spirit, joining our cry with his own.

How, then, could we picture the Father deaf, when our being, united to the Spirit of Jesus, speaks all the possible variations of the unique cry, "Abba," "Dad" (Romans 8:15)? The Father cannot refuse to listen to the desire of his own Son in this word, springing up in our hearts through the Spirit's intercession: the desire to be one with him as his sons and daughters, to be one with one another as brothers and sisters, the desire for a Person.

He cannot be deaf. He listens to all our cries as they express in the Spirit of his Son a desire that defines his own divine life: life shared by the three Persons of the Trinity, life given to us, life that is love. The Letter to James says in a very strange passage, "Do you think that the Scriptures say in vain, 'He desires with jealousy the Spirit he has given you'?" (James 4:5).

Paul says, "The proof that you are his sons is the fact that God sent forth into our hearts the Spirit of his Son which cries out 'Abba' (Father)" (Galatians 4:6). The proof that the Father can never be deaf is the fact that his Spirit cries out to him. "The Spirit himself joins our spirit in witnessing that we are God's children" (Romans 8:16). He cries out with us the overflowing love of the Son, Jesus; he cries out with Christ, "made our flesh" in all of us, the love of sons and daughters.

"In your prayer do not rattle on like the pagans. They think they will win a hearing by the sheer multiplication of words. Do not imitate them. Your Father knows what you need before you ask him," says Jesus (Matthew 6:7-8). Now we understand why we need not multiply words, thoughts or images; why we need not worry when we have none. Now we understand why everyone always prays: the Father always knows the deepest cry of our being, his "boy's cry" within each of us. The Father cannot help hearing and listening to our depths, for we are pregnant through the Spirit uniting us with his own Word. As it was in Mary, the Word is conceived and carried within us, and the Father cares for him lovingly.

Even though we do not hear it, we know our heart is beating. He knows, too, and he listens to it.

WE LIKE DEAFNESS IN GOD AND OURSELVES

We are sure the Father always listens to us, for he recognizes in our cries as sons and daughters, echoes of his own "boy's cry." Since from God's point of view our being prays unceasingly, we might be tempted to conclude that it is not necessary to express words verbally, nor images and thoughts mentally, for God reads our hearts. Indeed the question arises: why should we pray, set aside specific times, choose particular places, use certain bodily postures, use various methods, if God already knows what we need? The danger is to think that we might eliminate formal ways of praying, contrary to all the religious traditions. If the Father already listens to the deepest cries of our being, is it really important to externalize our prayer in forms that will in any case be too superficial?

Never would we deny the importance and benefit of any formal method of prayer. But we must look carefully at what we do with it. Sometimes we might use methods of praying in order to deafen the Lord and remain deaf ourselves.

CONCRETIZING OUR PRAYER LIFE

Let us briefly examine what happens when we concretize our prayer life: first, when we pray as a group, and second, when we pray by ourselves.

When we pray as a group

Reasons Because we want to become more *consciously* a religious group, we pray together in a visible manner. Through this common prayer we want to become more aware of God's inspirations so that we may *discern* what the Lord is saying to the group, in each individual member and through what we share with one another. Our discernment seeks to know God's will for all of us and helps us to assume our *responsibility* as a group, arriving at necessary collective decisions for the good of each person and of our common mission.

Thus we hope, each one of us, and all of us as a group, to express our *love* for the Lord, and our *faith* in what we are and what we have to do for God.

Outward behavior Common prayer necessarily has visible expression; people have to come together concretely. A kind of collective *silence* is already accomplishing something between the persons present.

- We knew that she would die soon. During our Eucharist with her, we listened to the Song of Songs, "Come now, my love, my beloved one..." We knew the words fit her; so we all remained silent.

- The inmate was on furlough. Together with him in the car, we silently enjoyed our communion outside the prison.

We must not renounce this intimacy too quickly, embodying as it does a truth so often forgotten. On the other hand, members of a group who seem to be one are often silently miles away from one another; but we cannot see this.

- After a long and silent ecumenical prayer session, I was attacked verbally about my faith by a person of another Christian denomination. Where was the apparent unity of our silent prayer?

God who listens to the heart knows whether in silence we are close to or far from one another. Our silence may conceal our divisions.

So in order to build the desired oneness, people involve their *bodies*.

- How many times my own prayer has been helped just by seeing the bodily postures of my brothers and sisters.

- The liturgical dance of the monks allowed us to enter more easily into their peaceful and joyful praise.

The feeling of union increases when all act in the same way with the body, as happens in any parade or gymnastic demonstration.

- During a retreat for prisoners, after we had washed one another's feet we realized that something had happened within each one of us, inmates and outsiders.

Afterward, however, we may become disillusioned to hear some participants admitting to internal distraction, escape or refusal.

- Many times during military parades we soldiers were more interested in looking at the girls, angry about the weight of our rifles, furious over the loss of a furlough, rather than celebrating the freedom gained on Bastille Day or the peace given us at the end of World War I or II.

The Lord is not deceived by the language of our bodies. He knows our interior attitudes; as a group we may not be aware of these, pretending that we are one.

When people really want to create intimacy, they go further. The desire to become one by sharing thoughts and feelings requires the use of *words.* Each one expresses verbally to the group what he or she thinks or feels.

- Only when we shared verbally about the washing of the feet in prison was it revealed as a moment of deep forgiveness, acceptance and love for one another: blacks and whites, Protestants and Catholics, women and men.

Sometimes communion requires that we all say the same words and sing the same songs. When the disciples said to Jesus, "Lord, teach us to pray," he gave them the words of the Our Father (Luke 11: 1-4). The rites and symbols used in celebrations are grounded partly in this need for a common expression.

But here again, words sometimes betray us, and we betray our words.

- We need not enumerate the many times our lips have sung the same songs in our churches while our hearts could not join in the common sorrow or joy.

- When we say the Lord's Prayer during our services, do we always mean what we say? For instance, "...as we forgive those who trespass against us"?

We cannot pretend that we perfectly express our depth and never lie. "This people draws near with words only and honors me with their lips alone, though their hearts are far from me," complained the Lord through Isaiah and Jesus (Isaiah 29:13; Matthew 15:8). The Lord cannot be deceived; but it is so good to cover up our feelings with words!

As members of a group we need to see and hear external *signs* in order to build communion. Each member must show himself and others signs of belonging to the group. The deaf and blind tell us how much they miss outward signs. But the limitations we have mentioned at the end of the preceding paragraphs, while not destroying the necessity and value of signs, show us their relativity and fragility. Since he reads our hearts directly, God does not need our signs and cannot be deceived by them. But since we human beings are not pure spirits, we cannot live without signs, even though we may use them to cover up our true feelings. When we give a certain form to our common prayer, then, it is really only for us, and not for the Lord, who does not need it. But we may close our ears to the signs, preferring deafness to the knowledge of our inner self that the Father possesses.

I might add here that when we do not want to see our feelings unveiled, we presume that their revelation would be too explosive and therefore dangerous for the group or ourselves, or we are simply afraid because we think such feelings shameful. So we pretend to be different and try to ignore them. Is it really that we are not sure about the love and faith of the Lord and the group?

When we pray by ourselves

Reasons As human beings we need to express our thoughts and feelings in order to become *conscious* of ourselves in our relationships, with our friends and with God. This is characteristic of humanity.

- It was a great turning point for the man when he dared to say aloud to God as he looked out on the ocean, "I love you."

This awareness is a necessity. It is my beauty and dignity to become a conscious person, in order to know and direct myself as much as possible. *Discernment* is the understanding and lucidity that show us who we are and where we must go. Based on this, our *responsibility* can make decisions according to who we are and what we have to do. The purpose of a systematic prayer life is to become a responsible person able to say "yes" to the Lord's call that defines our being and mission.

- I have discovered that I am called to share the Father's compassion for the poor. Now I can more willingly direct myself in the way I am to follow.

Through the external expression of our prayer we hope to show *love* to the Lord. It gives us the possibility of concretizing our attachment to him. A gentle word, a caress, a letter, a gift are concrete proofs of love. But what if the loved one does not need signs? They are proofs at least for the giver. We prove to ourselves that we love, showing the values and price we attach to the one we love. The same logic applies to our *faith*.

- A good spiritual master told me years ago, "When I pray, I prove to myself at the very least that I am able to waste time for the Lord."

Outward behavior When we pray we need to use visible signs in order to find out if we want to pray and if we actually do so. *Silence* may be one of these signs.

- She told me that, seized by Jesus' forgiveness of her, she could only remain silent.

We shall have the opportunity to come back to the question of silence; but is it not true that sometimes our silence is only the result of spiritual laziness or fear?

- He said, "I really do not know what it was. Was I spiritually slothful or did I refuse to open my door to the Lord? The fact is that I dozed."

God knows, of course, whether our silence means intimacy or not; We may sometimes wonder, "I am silent. Am I running away?"

In order to see whether or not we are with the Lord, we may use our *body* intelligently in prayer. Kneeling, standing, lying on the floor, prostrate, naked, concentrating on our breathing, we want to involve the whole of our being before the Lord. We refuse to divide ourselves into pieces and put some of them aside.

- The retreatant discovered that when she was lying on her bed she was inwardly given up to the Lord's action. It worked very well.

But the body may become a distraction that pulls us away from prayer.

- She wanted to pray on her knees for hours. But she could not pray because it hurt so much. Then she realized that it was an excellent excuse: the more it hurt, the less she was listening.

- He wanted to pray naked and made the decision by himself, without letting the Lord lead him. He became aware that he was really flattering his own sensuality.

If the Lord hears the deepest cries of our being, we sometimes substitute other cries in order to avoid listening. What are they?

We want to clarify our prayer, perhaps for discernment. So we use thoughts and *words*. Things are clearer when we can speak them. "What is clearly conceived is clearly enunciated," according to a poet.

- She understood how much she loved him when she found herself praying and interceding for him. Before that, she doubted the reality of her love.

- He had gradually stopped praying every day and going to services every Sunday. He admitted that his faith became weaker through lack of such signs. "Like love," he said.

We all know that the Lord does not need many words or thoughts. So why do we sometimes babble so much, with our minds working like computers?

- I remember a certain retreatant. Her retreat changed when she stopped thinking and talking a lot with me and with the Lord. With the flood of words gone, we discovered pearls on the beach.

What are we hiding behind the flood of our words and thoughts? What are we afraid to hear behind our questions and answers? Why do we try to deafen the Lord with constant noise?

As human beings we need signs of expression in order to establish and consciously develop our communion with the Lord. But the limitations we have mentioned, without diminishing the value of signs, reveal their dangers. *God does not need our signs.* But we cannot live without them. We may work with them in a very subtle way, contrary to their purpose and goal. They are means of communication. We change them into ear plugs in order to avoid communication or in order to falsify it. Worse, we sometimes try to "jam" the voice of the Lord with noise, like interference on the radio.

When we give a certain outward form to our prayer life, it is *only for ourselves*; the Lord does not need it, And we may use it in order to remain deaf and make God deaf too.

We may suppose that our masks forbid the revelation of our inner feelings for some reason. Would it be too explosive for us, too dangerous in our relationship with God? Are we not so sure of love and faith? Let us give here one answer; the rest will come later.

WHY DO WE PREFER TO REMAIN DEAF?

We are human beings, not pure spirits. As soon as anything occurs in our lives, it is immediately rooted and revealed in our flesh and bones. When something happens, our body registers it and emits signals. Our most intimate thoughts and feelings are registered and revealed by signs in our brain cells, our hormonal system, our muscles and nerves, our members and senses. Without this we could not live. When all signs disappear from life, it is time to die.

This necessity and the fact that signs are essentially for ourselves create an unavoidable self-centeredness in our use of them. This opens the door to our usual selfishness. So when we formalize our prayer and use signs, we may desire, think and feel it to be done for the Lord, but how much of it is for our own self-satisfaction or self-preservation?

Let us see.

In examining our misuse of signs, the first thing we see is our *spiritual greediness*. We try to hold on to, nurse and recreate the spiritual consolations we have formerly known because of their delicious flavor. More interested in the taste of his gifts, we forget the Giver and try to substitute ourselves for him. Through our own capacity for self-pity, we create warm, make-believe cocoons for ourselves. Even when the Lord purifies our love and faith, by allowing dryness to enter our prayer life, we greedily love ourselves before we love him and use him for self-gratification.

- The retreatant discovered that her so-called intimacy with Abba, the Father, was simply a very childish attitude. She understood this when she understood how absent Jesus was from her prayer life.

Concerned with our own self-satisfaction, we do not want to hear God's lesson, intended to help us grow and chew meat instead of eternally sucking milk. We do not want to hear the cry of our being that wants to be child-like but not childish forever.

Narcissism underlies spiritual greed, especially when the attraction for spiritual "sweets" is strong and lasting. If there is adoration, it is self-worship. The whole cosmos is focused on self; we are for ourselves the whole world. What appears to be a dialogue between the Lord and us is really a monologue. We mother ourselves in the worst fashion, being at the same time the baby. A spiritual schizophrenia may even occur through the magic of our words and thoughts: images and lullabies created by our need for self-gratification.

- He already knew that he had an exaggerated devotion to Mary, the mother of Jesus. As soon as he saw that he identified himself too easily with Jesus in the manger, he began to understand that it was very ambiguous.

We would rather be deaf than hear the Lord calling us to be adult persons present to the world, and we do not like to listen to the tensions between our physical growth and our retarded affective age. Perhaps we refuse to hear the Lord denounce ourselves as our own idols, or the depths within us desiring to reach out.

We realize that all our stratagems for self-satisfaction or gratification aim at our self-preservation. They are signs of an *escape*. We seem to build with God. In fact, we are building with ourselves a very private world of which we think we possess all the landmarks. There we feel welcome, accepted, recognized, warm and secure. It looks like a permanent summertime with self as the only sun, in perfect isolation.

* While he spoke about his prayer life, I never heard him say one word about anything concerning the world: family, business, nation, no mention at all. As soon as I started to wonder about this, his whole ivory tower collapsed.

We do not like to confront God's call sending us out to the world, dangerous and unknown as it is. We are reluctant to face that other unknown world—also dangerous—of the deepest levels of self. And finally, we are petrified by the thought of having to enter more deeply into the totally other world of God.

Here we can understand why we try to cover the Lord's voice and block his hearing with all the noises we create around ourselves. Not only do we hide what could come out of ourselves through his inspiration, but we do not want God to listen to what may be bubbling up within us. Such an unknown is so different, so strange, so difficult to control, that it terrifies us like a giant. We are like the people of Israel before the new land. We hear a frightening message: "The land that we explored is a country that consumes its inhabitants. And all the people we saw there are huge men, veritable giants...We felt like mere grasshoppers, and so we must have seemed to them." Even though hunger and thirst tell us, "We ought to go up and seize the land, for we can certainly do so," we say to ourselves, "We cannot attack these people, they are too strong for us" and we are ready to stay in the desert (Numbers 13:30-33). We even forget the "grapes...pomegranates and figs...and milk and honey" promised! (Numbers 13:23,27)

Thus we grasp that the key word of all this behavior is *fear*. Fear of the other, of the Other. And we do not want to listen to the cry of our being that desires encounter with them because it knows that it cannot survive without them. But God is listening to this depth.

To pass over to others is to dare to enter an unknown land for which we have no landmarks. Fearful of losing all our signs, the ones we think we know, we are afraid to confront death.

Signs are necessary in order to see if we have love and faith. Their misuse may make us doubt our sense of love and faith. In our prayer life do we believe that since God hears the deepest cries of our being, we must not deafen him, which, in fact, would be an impossible undertaking? Why then should we be afraid to let him hear our depths, and to let ourselves do the same, without fear, *with him?* Let us go with Joshua who heard the Lord saying to him, "I will deliver to you every place where you set foot...I will not leave you nor forsake you. Be firm and steadfast so that you may give this people possession of the land which I swore to their fathers I would give them...Do not fear nor be dismayed, for the Lord, your God, is with you wherever you go" (Joshua 1: 1-9). With his love we are able to face anything. If we believe that this listening God is a loving God, why should we be afraid to venture forth with his Word, even against giants? With David we can brave our inner and seemingly gigantic enemies, saying, "You come against me with sword and spear and scimitar, but I come against you in the name of the Lord of hosts...Today the Lord shall deliver you into my hand" (1 Samuel 17:45-46b).

A FORTUNATE FAILURE

Something may help us to risk the adventure: the very dangers and limitations of the signs. Indeed misuse of the signs usually leads to failure that may prove to be lucky.

Empty and prolonged silence makes us more and more restless until we can no longer stand it.

The first proof is precisely the inability to keep our body quiet and peaceful. As for multiplying words, thoughts and images too easily, this tires our head and gives us words that have no savor, thoughts that no longer nourish, and images that fade away in the twinkling of an eye. Unsuccessfully we have tried to satisfy our spiritual greediness: our accustomed food and drink are no longer enough to sustain us; a new hunger and thirst seize us. The false consolations we have given ourselves appear more clearly as daydreams without consistency. We are aware that the movie of which we are both director and star deserves no Academy Award. We aspire after space, suffocating because we have no company at the narrowest level of the world of self. We can no longer escape an increasingly insistent call. We start to desire Someone other and Somewhere else, for we have walked through all the methods of prayer and have found the most superficial parts of self. Even though we are tired, we long for another trip, for Someone new. And God is always new.

We feel more and more painfully that we need only the desired One who gives himself *through* signs but remains *beyond* them. We already know that we are dwelt in by one greater than we can spontaneously perceive. The life and love we know are the symptoms of a Life and Love far more astounding. We desire to discover all the Life and Love that can possibly be within us. We want a change of level.

We held in our fingers a pinch of sand, a drop of water, but we feel that we were made for all the beaches and all the oceans of the earth. Deep within we hear, "He took him outside and said: 'Look up at the sky and count the stars if you can'" (Genesis 15:5). Words of the promise, call to a journey.

And we yearn for the tide.

LISTENING TO OURSELVES WITH THE LORD

If we travel with the Lord, a beautiful Promised Land, the country of freedom, will be given to us, and no obstacle will keep us from conquering it. So let us go forth and try to listen to the deepest cries of our being as God does, with him. This chapter is intended to indicate a way that may help us on this journey.

We know now that we cannot avoid using signs in the adventure of prayer, and we know that this is good. But we can decrease the risks of misusing them. We have to find the fine line between keeping the advantages of signs and becoming trapped in the stratagems of our fears. Paul has given us an excellent piece of general advice that we may apply to our use of signs: we have to use the signs as though we were not using them (1 Corinthians 7:31).

David went into battle without Saul's weapons (1 Samuel 17:38-40), just as the small and weak person he was, but he fought with the help of God's word. Let us begin doing the same: as the persons we are, with God's Word. *"You gave me a body...here I am"* (Hebrews 10: 5-7).

Let us go first of all with the poverty and weakness of our body. We were reminded in the first chapter how vulnerable our body is to the emotions we feel deep within us. It is so vulnerable that it becomes very sensitive and cannot lie as easily as our mind can. Exaggerated control of the body is very ambiguous.

- I remember two retreatants. I did not have to question them about their inner freedom. A look at their bodily postures told me enough: one sat as though she were tied, legs always crossed, hands always clasped, with an everlasting smile like the Mona Lisa. She reminded me of standing at attention as I had done in the army. The other was exactly the contrary.

Such behavior clearly shows not the desire to channel bodily expression, but an unconscious attitude of repression. How can what is deepest within us come out? We have to act in such a way that we do not forbid the body to react. When it does, it "says" something.

That is why spiritual writers always invite us to be free with our body while praying. We take the posture that gives us the greatest spiritual freedom, the greatest help for our prayer. We do not fall into laziness, but we create a kind of relaxation that frees the body itself. The body will be ready to "talk" if necessary, and it gives freedom to the whole of our being.

- Someone gave me a good description of the result: "I had found the right posture: so much so that I did not feel my body."

But we have to go deeper than that. If all of a sudden we feel impelled to adopt a specific body posture, we should do so, even though we may not immediately understand the meaning of this desire. Refusing to do so may block something our depth wants to express, and then will certainly block the possibility of our becoming conscious of the message sent through the body but not yet decoded by the mind. I have seen many people make mistakes when they consciously decided to use the body in a certain way; I have never noticed failures when people followed their bodies' suggestions.

- He started in the fetal position and finished with all his members extended. According to what the body was saying, he had traveled a long way through his retreat: from childhood to adulthood.

- The first time she really understood deeply that she was a woman was when she touched her arms with her fingers.

Our body "speaks" our deepest feelings many times before our consciousness does. This is its weakness and vulnerability, but also its richness. When we forbid our body to talk, we put on a "tunic," a "bronze helmet," a "coat of mail" that does not fit us, as David did (1 Samuel 17:38-40). We are not who we are deep within; we are just building walls around ourselves and losing our freedom. It is better to go forth as we are, but with God's Word.

STARTING WITH THE SCRIPTURES

Some people think it is good to pray with our own thoughts and feelings alone, using nothing else. It may be good at times. But I think it is always better to start with Scripture. If I say "start," it is because only the starting point depends on us many times. The rest of our prayer depends on the movements of the Spirit within us. According to one translation, we have to "begin the work," and the Lord will fill our temple with his peace and glory, accomplishing all his promises (Haggai 2:1-9).

"Walk humbly with your God" (Micah 6:8)

Starting our prayer with the Scriptures helps us to avoid some of the dangers we have unmasked. Any kind of formalization hides the hazards of our fears, escapes, narcissism, and spiritual greed. Undoubtedly the risks are increased if we decide to start with our own conscious thoughts and feelings. If we begin with God's word, on the other hand, we give it a priority that already rejects the temptation to self-satisfaction. Our desire and love are directed to him.

We also give ourselves the strength we need to face our unknown fears, the force symbolized by David, as we mentioned before.

In addition, because we believe that the Word we use is guaranteed by God, starting with it is already an act of faith. We begin to confide ourselves to his own Word; therefore we trust in his love for us. There is no room for any fear of the Other; instead of fleeing from him, we go forth with him, no longer looking for self-preservation. And such an act of courage may already be a responsible, adult act of love.

It would be impossible to list all the people who have discovered a different kind of prayer and spiritual life as soon as they began to pray with the Scriptures.

"Do not rattle on" (Matthew 6:8)

We say that excessive words may jeopardize our contact with God. Talking too much to or about God is always ambiguous. So let us pray without a flood of words, verbal or mental. Let us believe in and ponder his own Word, giving priority to it over ours. There can be fear in too many words, also a lack of faith. Notice the brevity of the Lord's Prayer, as an example. Prayer life always grows simpler and simpler.

- The thirty-day retreatants see their written notes, their talks with the retreat master, their prayer time, gradually invaded by silence.

Above all, let us avoid thinking too much. Systematic analysis, rationalization, reasoning to a logical conclusion, are escapes that hide fear in a kind of utilitarianism that cannot accept having nothing. Praying more silently takes this away while it dissolves babbling and rattling on; and we start believing in action that he knows what we actually need.

- They were willing to be more silent when they heard Paul saying, "To him whose power now at work in us can do immeasurably more than we ask or imagine, to him be glory..." (Ephesians 3:20).

For this purpose it is helpful to know how to select the text we are going to pray with. We have to pray with passages which touch us with profound desire for them. More than our mind, our heart tells us what our depth needs. We must take only the Scripture passages that touch us and give us deep feelings. This does not mean praying with texts we like, but rather with those that create as deeply as possible an echo within us. Suppose that a text gives us interesting thoughts; as long as it does not touch us deeply, it has *nothing* to tell us. It may favor intellectual escape, but praying is not first of all an intellectual matter. And of course a text that remains "silent" should never be used for prayer.

A very good way

When we want to remove as much as possible the stratagems of our fears, it is good to pray with the imagination, the capacity to make images in the mind. It is usually easier to do so if we take scenes from Scripture which contain some action, at least at first, since discourses do not offer much to the imagination. We picture with our imagination the scene that touches us, we visualize the story told to us, just as if we were present as a witness. We see the streets of Jericho, Zacchaeus unable to see Jesus and then climbing the sycamore tree, the Lord going to his house (Luke 19). We put ourselves then into the scene either as an *actor* or as a *spectator*.

As a spectator we are anonymous, unnoticed but there, one of the crowd or one of the disciples, for instance. With our imagination we see what was done, we hear what was said, and we let the heart react as freely and spontaneously as possible. As an actor, we see if we can wear the shoes of one of the main characters, perhaps even Jesus, Mary or the Father. We do what he or she did, we say what he or she said, and once again we let our depth react as freely as possible. If the text channels the imagination through its objective description, then we cannot go anywhere; the free reactions of our heart give us back our freedom.

Let us now see what happens when we pray like this with the Scriptures.

THE GIFT OF THE SCRIPTURES

The whole of the Bible is in part an education of Israel by the Lord. He taught his people how to use the signs he gave them, emphasizing some and eliminating others according to the needs of the Jewish people at a specific moment of their history.

Praying with the Old Testament

When we pray with the Old Testament, we meet the persons who wrote the different books of the Bible and those they are writing about. Their word is a human word, but we believe that it says something true about God and about us. With our happy and unhappy experiences, with the whole of our lives, its passages send us to the experiences and lives of the writers or the ones written about. If we are deeply touched by the words we pray with, it means that something deep within us is in harmony with what the verses say to us. What the authors or their characters say about God and his relationship with his people— which is guaranteed to be divine revelation—provokes a kind of echo within us. A certain kinship exists between what is deep within us and the spiritual experience described in the text. Because something similar exists between the cry of our depth and the cry of the persons we meet in the words of the Bible, a kind of dialogue takes place between our hearts and the hearts of the writer or the people he is writing about. Our depth recognizes itself in the scene and starts to react spontaneously and freely At the same time our deepest desires are supported, nourished, developed and possibly healed by the partner we have encountered. Because the text tells us the truth of the situation recounted, the truth according to God's revelation, a certain truth about our own situation, truth according to God, is revealed within us, freed in us.

Sometimes this intercourse between our depth and the text is such a liberation that our cry, helped by the persons we have met in the Bible, passes through the doors of our being and appears clearly to our consciousness. As soon as we become aware of what we heard, we are able to deal with our own cry in a more responsible manner.

- Through the Song of Songs, he realized more clearly his deep desire to risk himself as a loving and loved person.

- With Hagar (Genesis 16 and 21), this woman understood how greatly her spiritual life had been influenced by her competitive relationship with her mother.

But sometimes what happens within us cannot be clearly understood, like a musical composition with which we identify without knowing why. Something has happened deep within our being. In prayer we may experience the same thing: consolation, contentment, peace and joy tell us of the advent of a liberation, but we remain totally unable to express exactly how, why and what.

- She does not know why Elijah attracts her in 1 Kings 19; she only knows that after praying, she feels strong enough to go on with her life.

- He did not feel anything spectacular while praying with David fighting against Goliath, just very much at home. But some days later, he found himself fighting easily with the gigantic problems he had to solve.

Praying with the New Testament

All the things we have described in regard to the Old Testament find their deepest expression when we talk about the New Testament, whose texts all concern Jesus. Of course for Christians, the Old Testament also speaks about Jesus, for this was the Scripture that Jesus prayed with; it was his "roots" and announced him through figures and symbols. But we may understand more clearly what is happening when we pray with the Scriptures if we look at the New Testament.

Let us first remember what Jesus promised.

> I have much to tell you, but you cannot bear it now. When he comes, however, being the Spirit of truth, he will guide you to all truth. He will not speak on his own, but will speak only what he hears....In doing this he will give glory to me, because he will receive from me what he will announce to you. All that the Father has belongs to me. That is why I said that what he will announce to you he will have from me (John 16:12-15).

The Spirit of Jesus reacts within our depth when we pray with the Word of Christ, or the Word about Christ, the Son of God. The experience we described with the Old Testament takes place here too, but this time it is connected with the Son of God, the "pattern" of each one of us. When our inner depth is touched by a text that recounts an experience of sonship similar to our present one, it is like the essence of two radio waves: the Word finds and produces an echo within our heart. The Spirit of Christ within us echoes what happened to Jesus or to the persons in contact with him. A vibration created by the harmony between the situation of Jesus or someone influenced by him and our own spiritual situation is set up. The similarity of the two situations resonates at the deepest level of our being, precisely where the image and likeness of Jesus resides, precisely where we are a son or daughter of the same Father, possessed by the same life and love.

The cry of the Son, or about him in the text, enters into harmony with the cry of the son or daughter that we are and reveals something about it. Guaranteed by the fact that it is the Son's Word, the "pattern's" Word, it reveals something true about the son or daughter we are right now. Our cry of desire is clarified, nourished, and freed by the perfect cry of the Son echoing within us.

A recognition takes place. Praying with the situation described in the New Testament, my inner self recognizes itself more clearly in the words and actions of Jesus the Son, and the text about him becomes a text about me. This recognition tells me something about who I am right now, and I may grow in awareness of my current identity as a son or daughter of the Father. What is said about the Son is said about me. I am the one the text unveils and reveals.

- I recognized myself in the agonizing Christ: I have to say a painful "yes" to a very difficult decision.

- Chapters 8 and 9 of Matthew describe Jesus—and me. Recently I have given myself so much to people, healing them through my words and deeds.

Sometimes this kind of revelation reaches the conscious level so powerfully that the person is surprised by the truth it carries within itself. This is perhaps the best example I have ever seen:

- A very old Carmelite sister had tried to pray as I have described. After a while, she heard herself using the intimate form of address to God. (*Tu* in French, "thou," implies a more intimate relationship than *vous*, "you.") She later explained how surprised she was, since she had never used the intimate form with God in her prayer life. Her deepest self had treated God with more loving desire than her conscious expression.

This recognition is not always grasped on the conscious level. Nevertheless, the kinship, echo, and resonance between ourselves and the New Testament situation are so authentic that our being cannot help reacting. The harmony of the deepest level of ourselves with the text is perceived in the consolation, peace, joy, tears and/or contentment which seize us—the strong positive feelings—even though no intellectual understanding is given to the mind.

- Several times a week for three years, he prayed with the Transfiguration of Jesus, so powerful was the attraction of the text for him. This prayer always gave him deep peace. Why? How? Finally he understood.

Our heart, our inner depth, is groaning with pleasure while the head does not know why. Is this the "groaning" of the Spirit mentioned by Paul in Romans 8? Perhaps. just as lovers can only groan when they are grasped by the intensity of their love surpassing what is happening in and through them; if they feel a great contentment and fulfillment, they can only enjoy it without being able to express it clearly. Something good and surprising has happened to them, but it cannot be expressed in words or concepts.

The well-being we feel means that we are really at home praying with this text that so perfectly matches our present spiritual situation. We should stay with it in order to allow it time to free whatever desire is waiting to come forth from our depths.

So when we are confronted with the Scriptures working as we have described, we might say that the text operates as a catalyst. The spiritual situation matches our spiritual state; so our projection on the screen provided by the text takes place very easily. (We might remark in passing that if we simply create a void within ourselves, nothing can happen because we have no screen for any projection.) A phenomenon of catharsis occurs. What dwells within us identifies with one of the characters in the scene and may develop all, or at least some, of its potentialities. The scriptural spiritual experiences act like the sun, which through its warmth enables a rosebud to unfold its petals, manifest its beauty, and exude its perfume.

We do not always understand all the dimensions of the phenomenon, but we "know" that something is freed within us. Why is this an experience of freeing? Because something repressed or hidden that has been behind the scenes for years is finally released and at times raised to the conscious level. Remember the Carmelite sister's love finally becoming conscious. I firmly believe that this liberation is powerfully assisted by our faith and hope. The whole undertaking is accomplished under the sign of faith and hope in an unconditional Love, the Lord himself. We believe that through prayer we enter into the presence of such Love, with his Word present in the Scriptures given us by the Church and with his Word present in the depths-of ourselves given by his Spirit. This faith leads us to hope for everything possible (Luke 1:37). It removes shame and guilt feelings with the certainty of perfect forgiveness. It prohibits despair and fatalism through the belief that love is stronger than any kind of death. It even creates an attraction for the unknown because of the awareness that the Giver is always greater than any of his gifts. In brief, we can say that this sort of experience may happen because there is "no room for fear in Love" (I John 5:18).

- "What has kept me going during this retreat is the fact that I have always seen you deeply convinced that a fantastic power of Love was present in me. Your faith and hope gave me faith and hope," she said to me.

- "If I were not sure that I am a child who is heard, I would never be here," was her summary.

THE PROMISED LAND

Usually the more we silence our words, our thoughts, our images, and the quieter our body becomes, the more effective are the texts of the Scriptures, the deeper is the liberation worked within us when we pray. We enter slowly into another land, the Promised Land spoken of by all spiritual writers.

Let us use the imagery of the Bible. As soon as, and as long as, we pray as we have indicated, we enter into our new land, discovering and hearing the deepest cries of our being with the Lord. Enemies appear, like the "Amorites, Perizzites, Canaanites, Hittites, Girgashites, Hivites and Jebusites" but they are "delivered into our power" by the hand of God (Joshua 24:11-12). Cries that hinder or weaken life and love within us fade away or are no longer dangerous. Allies appear to make the life and love possible within us burst into bloom. And we feel that we are going deeper and deeper to the center of our being, as the Jews found their Holy City, Jerusalem. There we discover our source, our Temple, the sanctuary of life and love from which "rivers of living water shall flow" (John 7:38; Ezekiel 47).

Our prayer progressively emphasizes more and more the presence of the One who creates the echoes we have talked about, echoes of the Word about Jesus and the Father. We are less and less interested in what we discover, more and more concerned with our Guide himself. The Spirit becomes the center of our attention. Step by step we are seized by his presence, by the love within us, more and more in wonder before him. Instead of looking at the poor drop of love trickling out of us, instead of seeing the dams we build that diminish the amount of water flowing through us—exercises in futility that result in despair after a time—we contemplate all the love possible within us. The fierce current, the deep river, the limitless ocean of love is the subject of our inner contemplation, and we are led to silent and loving reverence. In our Holy of Holies, love is so lovable!

Our own word becomes silent and gives total priority to the Spirit's Word within us. We withdraw from the stage. We let our guest, the Spirit, say, do, and desire what it wants. At last all the possible love we contain can express itself freely in our being. Slowly, gradually, the same will be true of all our actions, more effectively than could ever have been possible through our own poor and self-centered efforts. Even though ascetical practices may remain, asceticism definitively gives way to our mystical vocation.

Slowly the Spirit's work takes place in us, the dialogue between the Father and the Son, their mutual love and desire. Within us God can finally listen to and enjoy his own song of life and love. Unable to remain inside, it overflows of itself into our lives. We are then, as sons and daughters, authentically who we are: the Temple of the Spirit of God, in Paul's words (1 Corinthians 6).

This mysterious divine dialogue is God's dialogue in us; it is not our own. We are no longer the hosts, but the guests, of the three Divine Persons. Paradoxically, however, it is also our own, for we are really the sons and daughters we are called to be, on whom his favor rests (Mark 1: I 1), upon whom the Spirit descends, overshadowed by the power of the Most High (Luke 1:35).

Deep down we savor an exceptional silence, a repose difficult to describe, of which we know nothing while knowing something. Sometimes we feel more distinctly an invasion of awe, praise, and thanksgiving. We see the fruit of the presence freed to act in our daily life: the fruit of life and love, with a peace not easily disturbed by external events (though the slightest infidelity to love is immediately detected by us). We may even walk in a night like the dark side of a cloud; though it was dark, it led them in their exodus (Exodus 12), a sign of the Lord showing himself as the one he is: always present but unknown. Indeed, the deepest levels of freedom, life and love are always "beyond"...like the ocean behind the tide.

"I WILL LEAD HER INTO THE DESERT AND SPEAK TO HER HEART" (Hosea 2:16)

The imagery of the exodus of God's people helps us to symbolize our experience in the life of prayer. This is to be expected, since we always share in our spiritual journey the stages experienced by Israel in its history. So, as the Jews entered the Promised Land and ended their long journey in the Temple of Jerusalem centuries later, we are invited to enter into ourselves until we reach the seat of our deepest cries where the Spirit meets our spirit.

The Hebrews' adventure started with the crossing of the Red Sea and the Jordan. This act of courage and faith contained in itself all the steps that followed, so much so that God's people always remembered and celebrated the going out from Egypt as their founding experience. The beginning contained in fact the whole journey. The rest was enfolded within the departure and was revealed by history at the appointed time. Israel became more and more conscious that its exodus was to be constant, leaving "somewhere" and going "somewhere else" in order to discover and praise the ever-new life and love of a liberating God.

FROM THE BEGINNING

Why not try something equivalent in our prayer life? The journey we have described, which leads us to the Promised Land within us, has a starting point that may contain all the following stages, at least as seeds that have to grow, as potentialities that have to be revealed.

Let us sum up the purpose of this last chapter. According to what we have said, the Promised Land of our spiritual journey is a silence we must never obstruct, so that the three Persons within us may have the joy of being the hosts. This last part of the book asks, why not start our prayer life with a silence we never repress?

For all spiritual writers, prayer slowly passes beyond signs while still using them. Why not try from the beginning to do this: to use necessary signs to the extent that this is unavoidable, but as little as possible? We may begin praying by doing the least possible in order to give the Lord the freedom to do as much as he can and wishes. We have seen the value of formalization for our prayer; even though the results may seem superficial compared with what might be revealed of our depths, they are good at least as an attempt to express something. Articulation in itself is already something worthwhile. But why not try to save time and go farther and faster beyond the starting point? This is possible if we immediately distance ourselves from materialization of our prayer, of which we have considered the risks. Instead of rushing toward new methods of prayer, why not use a minimum and then start with silence? Instead of taking a pinch of sand or a drop of water, let us dare to possess the whole beach and swim in the ocean itself. This is not only our deepest desire; it is the Lord's as well. We are going to describe this suggestion in the present chapter, for we have seen it realized easily enough. The fruits were so amazing that we think it useful to propose such a way.

Such a proposal responds in fact to the deep desire of many persons who are suffering from many "noises" today.

In our societies, in one degree or another, noise reigns as king. We live on top of and among engines and motors always in action, for we have to produce constantly. We are assaulted twenty-four hours a day by the media...and we long for silence. More important still, our societies make a lot of "noise" about things not essential to life and love, or they disparage beautiful things as though they were wares to be sold, reducing them to just another "noise" among a thousand insignificant ones. We wait for silence to take away the empty messages and give deserved space to nourishing ones. And finally, our societies, characterized as they are by the power of the means of communication, keep us from communicating with one another and with ourselves because of all the "noise" that acts as permanent interference between human beings. We are hungry and thirsty for encounter with our brothers and sisters, with ourselves, in silence. Through ourselves and others we yearn for the Other, encountered only in his silence. Rebelling against the "noises" that hide the depths of others and of ourselves, we are starving for the silence of human and divine companionship.

How many among us are suffering from the noise of today? How many of us are afraid to be reduced to a superficial noise like a "noisy gong, a clanging cymbal" (1 Corinthians 13: 1)?

The desire for silence reinforces the wish to go farther and faster from the beginning. We must not waste time, for society does not wait to launch its attacks against us. Let us explain what we intend to suggest, hoping that we win satisfy such a wish and believing that it is possible to do so from the very beginning of our prayer life.

INITIAL SILENCE

Let us decide to start with Scripture in silence, expressing in fact all the elements of our faith. Step by step we shall describe the dimensions and benefits of this initial silence.

If we decide to start with silence, we immediately free ourselves from such questions about our prayer life as, "What stage am I at? Am I praying as long and as seriously as I should? What stage of spiritual growth am I now experiencing? What is the level of my holiness? Am I good enough?" The choice of silence already rids us of the selfish temptation to focus on our deeds and merits. Our decision to begin in silence removes the tendency to utilitarianism: using God through being greedy for immediate results, tangible gains and successes. Our initial silence nips in the bud our tendency toward self-satisfaction. Our inclination toward self-preservation is also affected. We insert a wedge into the protections we build, creating a gaping crack. But in order to be the one we say we are, this initial silence must be structured and particularized.

An act of faith with a minimum of signs

We cannot totally do without signs. But let us reduce them to a minimum, so that they will not become a coat of armor that keeps us from breathing and suffocates us.

As a screen for our imagination we might use the scene of the boy's cry in Genesis 21:14-17. Visualizing a thirsty child in the desert does not offer too much to the imagination; there is no risk of making a great movie. Or we may identify ourselves with one who is pregnant: Mary, for instance, as the one who was pregnant with the Word, without using any specific Scriptural passage. She is there, but lack of information about her pregnancy may dry up the source of our dreams.

If we are talkative and need words, we may repeat when necessary, words inspired by John 1 or Romans 8: "The Word made my flesh," "The Spirit groans within me." The "me" makes the passage more personal and fits the fact that *I* am the one praying now. Or we may use in the same way, "All my desire is before you, Lord," "The Word is already near me, already on my lips, already in my heart," from Psalm 38 or Romans 10:8.

We should not use all these passages, but only those touching us deeply, going back to them when we see ourselves getting away from behavior in faith. The question is not first of all to pray *with* the texts mentioned, but to use them as words or images *that give structure* to our act of faith. We repeat the words, we go back to the images, in order to assert quietly what we believe when we want to remain silent.

As a matter of fact, if we want to start with an initial silence and remain with it, if we want to use as few signs as possible, it is because we wish to assert to ourselves and to the Lord that we believe communication already exists between him as a listening Father and his own Word present in us. It is because we do not want to interfere with it that we avoid making ourselves and him deaf, and we allow this communication to be as it is, as the Lord wants it to be. With a minimum of signs, trying to be as silent as possible, we repeat only an act of faith, which signifies, "Lord, I believe in your presence within me, as the Word of your Spirit. I am sure your Word is mine, and mine yours. I believe that you, Father, are already talking with this Word and that he is talking with you. I do not want to disturb your dialogue as Father and Son in the same Spirit, for I am united to it. I refuse to impede your mutual desire to reach each other. I give you absolute priority; do whatever you want." And the words and images we have cited bring us back to this act of faith when necessary. But silence prevails, for it is in itself the whole of our act of faith.

Formerly we were taught to begin our prayer by placing ourselves in the presence of God; but his presence was almost always understood as something outside us. Here we do the same thing, but we know that his presence is actually inside us. We try simply *to be*, letting go of all unnecessary words, thoughts and images, keeping only the bare minimum. Just *being* is already a prayer.

Just being who we are, as human beings, temples of the Spirit, is already a hymn of praise to our Creator. So the silence of being present is a constant and beautiful prayer, centered on the One living within us, on his mysterious dialogue with the Father, devoid of narcissism and self-absorption. We worship and give thanks because we believe that someone lives within us, and we are grateful for it.

Living our pregnancy and waiting for delivery

We have to wait. Patiently we wait, accepting our pregnancy. It does not matter whether or not we are aware of anything; we believe that our being always prays, and that is enough for a believer.

- She was physically exhausted. Praying in silence, she found herself relaxed, consoled by the assurance that communication already existed between the Father and herself.

In such an initial silence is great vulnerability. We are totally given up to God's will in abandonment of self to his actions and his pleasure, through an act of love sure of his Love. It is also readiness. We are ready for delivery, ready for a clear revelation at the conscious level, but also ready to let the Lord continue the kind of talk he wants to carry on with himself within us. We are ready for any sort of "Ephphatha" (Mark 7:34). As a matter of fact we are so ready that our readiness is already an openness. We treat the three Persons as the hosts and allow them to do whatever they like.

The openness implied in our initial silence signifies a freedom and trust in God's love that will prepare without fear a way of liberation for our inner depth. Sure of his presence and confident in him in silence and abandonment, we do the least possible to satisfy the human need for signs. We believe what is most important takes place at another level, and thus we give the Lord the opportunity to do as he wishes in the depth of ourselves.

To some people this seems like nothing. But when they try it, they will see that it is not as easy as it looks. Persons who like to "rattle on" or who enjoy an "easy" prayer cannot stand this initial silence filled only with faith. Of course, there is a fantastic exodus here. Confident with the Lord as the Jews were with Moses and Joshua, we leave the country we know—the country of all the "noises"—for an unknown land. We go out of the land of so many forms of slavery: self-adoration, self-satisfaction, self-preservation. We refuse to be blinded by fear, and we are ready to face anything—even giants! We do not escape any unknown, our own or the Other's.

Listening to our body, letting our desires surface, we wait for the tide of our depth to flow out under the Spirit's guidance. We are ready for anything.

In such a silence everything is already given, just as it is with a child abandoned to his father, his "Abba."

GIFTS OF THE TIDE

- She summarized very well the *first* feelings we get in silence when we succeed in not repressing it: "I feel within myself some things that wanted to live and that I had not been attentive to."

This kind of silent prayer is not seeking action, profit, or visible effectiveness. It gives priority instead to receiving and being fashioned, to giving freely without return. It is cautious about the complications of formalization and skeptical about methods. We might say that it is like a fast from anything we ourselves could bring to our prayer life, a fast that opens us in faith and love to the gifts of the Lord; and often he brings "things that wanted to live" and that we had not listened to.

When the tide within us is released by the Lord, when it comes in (and I believe it always does), the gifts may be diverse, revealing themselves in ways like the following.

1. We are unaware of anything on the conscious level. We feel only a deep and silent peace. On other levels we get the impression that nothing is happening at all. Although time usually passes at a good rate of speed, it is, as a friend of mine used to say, "gently boring." But it is bearable.

2. Something is definitely happening, and the conscious level registers strong feelings, as if every passion were loosed. Hatred, anger, resentment, revolt, erupt violently within us, like a flood over a broken dam. Our prayer is far from boring; rather, it is overwhelming and frightening because of these "negative" feelings.

3. We experience the power of an explosion of "positive" feelings. Love and compassion, care and concern, gratitude and praise, awe and wonder, well up from our depth with overpowering force. We cry, our heart beats faster, our body trembles, we feel warm. It seems that a tidal wave carries us away and that we cannot resist. Sometimes it is so unbelievable that it is frightening: like death, "like an orgasm," as someone told me some years ago.

4. Something else may happen, but it is so difficult to describe it in words that I prefer to cite an encounter that impressed me.

- This man tells me that his heart is divided between two loves. He is very much in love with his wife and strongly attracted to his secretary. His mind, heart and body are happy and fulfilled with each of the two women at the same time. Because he is convinced about fidelity, he cannot love his coworker. He does not want to hurt either of his loves, but he is torn apart. After praying silently, he feels like a battlefield on which a fierce struggle rages, like a swimmer submerged and tossed about by opposing waves.

These are possible gifts of the tide, revealed by the Lord. These gifts may become graces if we stay with the act of faith included in our initial silence.

NOTHING APPEARS

When nothing reaches the conscious level and nothing seems to be happening, we feel as though we are in a desert. We have not artificially created a void; it creates itself. It is like the ebbing of the tide. If we stand fast with the faith of our initial silence, we learn—and more quickly than through the slow process of formalization—a great deal that is essential for a mature and responsible believer in regard to prayer and the

spiritual life. So we may save time, we may detect
and escape the traps that lie in wait for us.

Revelations

If nothing appears, we may think that our
inner resistance is too strong and admit it humbly.
But generally a person who resists cannot stay
with silence; something always happens.

We first learn to confront our fear of emptiness and to handle what we lack. This purifies
spiritual greed and all the things it hides. For instance, narcissism is eliminated, for the company
of self is not gratifying. No lasting spiritual intro-
spection can resist such a dry land.

Therefore we learn how to love, for we give
freely, getting nothing in return, nothing that we
can see. We waste our time for the Lord. We live
agape, love according to the New Testament, love
that is not primarily feeling empathy for someone
but acting for the good of the one we love. We finally understand the difference between liking
and loving.

- A man from Germany is in a coma, hospital-
  ized in Lyon, France. His wife comes from
  Germany. Though she knows not a word of
  French she stays beside his bed for weeks,
  day after day, night after night. She takes
  care of him in an awful loneliness, with doc-
  tors and nurses in admiration at such a love.

God and self assume their proper place. God is God, and we can no more master him in our depths than we can anywhere else. He shows up when he likes. We learn the spiritual poverty that is already a perception of the "beyond" that is God. We become aware of the message faster than through the usual formalization. Even when the Lord gives signs in order to tell us something about himself, he is always beyond all signs. The signs given to Israel expressed something about Yahweh, but at the same time they had to be gone beyond or lost: the Promised Land, the Kingdom, Jerusalem, the Temple and the Law, for instance. Even the Sign par excellence, Jesus himself, had to disappear (John 16:7).

We learn how to die to former signs in order to be open to receiving new ones. We learn death and resurrection from the beginning of our prayer life.

We have the strength and courage to face all the fundamental spiritual experiences, and the patience to hope for the Good News to come: this is faith. We are willing to go into the desert; for we believe that, even if the Word does not yet appear on our lips, it is already speaking within our heart (Hosea 2:16). We move forward, knowing that we "pray unceasingly."

Communions

Our initial silence forbids us to flee the world: ourselves, others, and the Other, God. When we let the experience engulf us, we are led to a deep communion with all people who are silent or voiceless in history. Even though we do not like to enter such company, we feel ourselves becoming one of them.

We become persons who cannot express anything, and we taste the suffering of this incapacity. We may tell God of our desire for expression, with the powerlessness of people on welfare for generations, of political prisoners, of masses without rights. We suffer with those who desire lovingly to share the ordeal of losing a child, the plight of an innocent person condemned to prison, of a friend who has had a nervous breakdown, of someone separated from his or her lover—of Jesus on his way to the cross.

- In the prayer group, someone began speaking about the terrible misery of the people in an underdeveloped country. I was shocked to hear the leader interrupt by singing loudly, "Christ is risen. Alleluia!"

We are Jesus' companions in his silence during the Passion, and we accept being companions of all the silent ones of the world.

On the other hand, we are numbered among those whose happiness is too great, and therefore speechless.

Who has not experienced the inability to express joy, gratitude or praise for a difficult birth, a painful creation, an unanticipated achievement? The person who never has cannot understand what I mean.

If the apparent nothingness of our initial silence impels us to ask God for the ability to express ourselves, it also puts us in communion with all those who beg God to hear. "God, please speak to me."

First, with those who realize they are deaf to the world and God.

- He has retired as an executive and has begun to contact volunteers working in the "Fourth World." He wrote to me, "How could I have been so deaf and blind all these years? I never imagined that such unbelievable misery could exist a few blocks from my home."

But we may also be among those who suffer from blocking the approach to God and others, among those more or less unbelieving people who honestly try to seek God and hear nothing.

- The young couple told me, "We feel that something will be missing in our commitment to each other if we have no religious ceremony for our wedding. But what exactly? Please help us in our search."

Finally, we may suffer in the name of those who are totally unconscious of the mistakes they are making, of the harm inflicted on themselves and others.

- Accused of murder, rape and robbery, he does not know what he has done.

Thus we may say, "God, please speak to me" with many others. Our communion extends to the point that they ask painfully, "Please, God, tell me about yourself."

We may already understand the people who implore the Lord, "Please teach me joy, peace and love. " But we may be able to relate more directly to the many persons who live the mystery of the beyond. People left alone, for instance, struggling "till the break of dawn" like Jacob with Someone, and groaning, "I will not let you go until you bless me....Do tell me your name, please" (Genesis 32:23-32).

- Only silence will enable me to understand the words of a friend of mine who is a hermit: "God has put within me such a thirst for love that I will never be happy as long as I have only crumbs of his presence. I must be given the whole loaf. Before this happens, we have to give all the blood of our heart in patience, in distance, to beg for love and give our heart to love so that he can love through us."

So when we let our silence deepen us, we know communion beyond words, thoughts, and images with the persons we have met in the examples used in the first part of this book. At the ultimate point of this communion, we are one with the silent desires of handicapped, insane, comatose and dying persons. Beyond fear of being forgotten and rejected, we commit them and ourselves to a silence where nothing and nobody can be lost, where Somebody hears and expresses the inexpressible. Where God/Love says to God/Love what only God/Love listens to. Where God utters himself as joy or suffering, through "my beloved son" and "Abba."

"NEGATIVE" FEELINGS

We really need the act of faith of our initial silence to be able to face the depth of ourselves when the tide has gone out and many signs with it. But how much more must we not call on our faith when suddenly the tide comes in and carries with it what are often seen as "bad" feelings. It is with reluctance that I call these feelings "negative." As soon as we make a judgment, we are led back to our fears through shame and guilt. We close the doors to liberation, so frightened are we.

Our fears

We do not want to allow anger, resentment, revolt, jealousy, envy, hatred and other "negative" feelings to come out. We more or less consciously refuse to listen to them, for they frighten us when they erupt with the violence of a volcano or the stubbornness of a migraine. We do not know what to do with them and how to handle them. Generally in our societies, the kind of education received in family, social and religious life does not help us to deal with such feelings; their expression has been punished so severely that we grow used to repressing them. They have always shown up, of course, but in various disguises: gluttony, authoritarianism, false humility, flattery. We thought we were rather good; so hearing them abruptly without ear plugs is frightening. Are they going to overpower us and escape our control? Will they hurt someone, starting with ourselves? They are so noisy and persistent.

- The retreatant told me what her day had been like. When I pointed out one single word in the margin of her written summary, a word she had not said in all her verbal descriptions, she was startled. The word was violence. For the first time the word and the feeling came out in her spiritual experience.

We try to cover up the howling or insidious voices of the feelings that frighten us most, the ones we do not want to listen to. These are the giants that seem to prowl "like a roaring lion looking for someone to devour" (1 Peter 5:8). We flee from them with fear, in self-preservation.

When we cease to be blind, we see that part of our depth unmasked, and we want to save ourselves from the teeth of shame and guilt. Fashioned by the standards learned and accepted from childhood, we cannot believe ourselves so ugly, and we do not want to feel the bite of guilt. Suppose people should discover who we actually are behind the facade. We are still afraid of being rejected as naughty children, just as we once were; and some sermons have reinforced this. We cannot help projecting on today the childish terrors of yesterday: the terror of rejection by everyone, including God, the terror of remaining lonely and lost forever. Paralyzed by the thought that the Lord might know the horrible truth of our being, we even attempt to make him deaf, as if he could not hear the cries within us!

The First Letter to Peter tells us, "Resist him, solid in your faith," referring to the roaring lion we have mentioned. We can if we cling to the belief underlying our initial silence; and we will not be disappointed with what will be revealed.

Revelation of the disfigured Christ

When we give our depth freedom to express this part of itself, our first gift is liberation from our fears. Let us suppose that those "bad" feelings are enemies. At least they are now known—and an identified adversary is less dangerous than a hidden one. Knowledge removes fear and gives us ninety per cent of the victory. We will no longer be led unconsciously. I have never found a retreatant who was not able to cope with such a discovery. Accepting those feelings as our own places us beside God, who had accepted them for so long without disowning us.

At last we share with God the revelation of our truth, and the truth will set us free (John 8:32). Yes, we are such people, experiencing such feelings. We say good-bye to the idol we have built; the sentimental hero or saintly person we dreamed we were is dead. It will henceforth be more difficult to be for ourselves a "father of lies" (John 8:44).

- "Father, how can you think that it is possible to hate God?"
  "Don't you ever have any harsh feelings against anyone, Sister, maybe even against God?"
  "Never."
  "You've been lucky," were my last words.

If we do think that we are sinners because of our feelings, that we are saying "no" to love, then we can acknowledge this and no longer say, "We have never sinned," making him "a liar" (1 John 1: 10). We can still pray as sinners to the one who came "to call not the righteous ones but sinners" (Matthew 9:13), to the one who died for us (Romans 8:2). Listening to our depth with him, we hear his words of forgiveness, and we learn to be merciful to ourselves, as he is to us. Sinners among sinners, we share the cries of all of them within us.

Then we are impelled to give all those feelings over to him. "All I have is yours"(John 17: 10), even those, we must admit in humility. We surrender ourselves to his salvation, believing more deeply still in a Lord who has mastered all the powers of darkness through his Christ. The faith of our initial silence is immediately challenged to grow deeper and deeper without delay; and our love will only increase through this experience.

It is undoubtedly a death for us to leave our pedestal. But if we get rid of the false image of ourselves, if we allow it to be destroyed by the tide of those feelings, we will be able to discover the true and lovable one.

We have spoken many times about the cries within us being assimilated with the groanings of the Spirit. But can we still do so when we speak about the kind of feelings we are dealing with now? This would be rather difficult. Here we are invited to discern what is "beyond." When a patient screams, we know he needs a sedative. When a child makes a scene, we know she is looking for attention. When workers strike, it is for better salaries or working conditions. In these situations we can see beyond what appears on the surface. Let us do the same with the faith of our silence. If we believe that the Word is present within us, then maybe our "bad" cries have something to do with him. And indeed they have, as we see when we go "beyond" these feelings.

Our disfigured face of Christ

We are sons and daughters of the Father, therefore Christ-like. But the face of the Son in us has been disfigured and wounded by the consequences of sin: the sins we have committed that have injured us deeply; the sins of our environment that have profoundly affected our past. What we have suffered as children from our parents, for instance, or grave physical diseases, or social disorders—injuries that so easily make us today jealous, angry, rebellious and hateful. Beyond our "negative" cries, we become aware of the disfigured face of a son or daughter of the Lord, of a brother or sister of all human beings, a face that desires and pleads for healing.

The cries we allow to surface through our initial silence reveal—and more quickly than through the usual route—not only that we must bring our sinful selves back to the forgiving mercy of the Father, but also that we must be the Good Samaritan for ourselves (Luke 10), and give over to the Father's care the disfigured persons we are.

Listening to the depth of ourselves with the Father, we are no longer afraid of our "negative" cries. Beyond them we hear the cries of a wounded person. Looking farther than the torture, of ourselves and of others, we see the victim. Then in our hearts we can share the tender compassion of the Father for the crucified one in us, for the Crucified One.

And so we are finally listening to our depth as Abba, our Father, always does.

- How many times I have said, "You are the first one, and in a sense the only one, who has to take care of the wounded child still present in you. You are for this injured child the love of the Father." And it has always been healing.

Communion with the disfigured ones

When we give our initial silence the opportunity to reveal the disfigured face of Christ in us, we will obviously be impelled to be one with all the disfigured ones of the world.

How can we now reject the people we do not like because they frighten us? Sometimes they make us fearful because they act as a mirror that reflects the face of ourselves that we do not want to recognize. We can no longer ostracize or excommunicate a violent person as easily as we formerly did, because we carry within us a part of the world's violence. In our depth we may be a Roman soldier, a Pharisee or a Scribe, Caiaphas or Pilate, Peter or Judas. We have our part in the passion of our time.

We enter into the communion of sinners, all descendants of the same Adam (Romans 5:12-21). But we are also in communion with the world that the Father does not condemn, but which he wants to save through his Son (John 3:17). How fortunate we are! If we did not need salvation, where would we be? We would not know our Savior Jesus. Our initial silence helps us very quickly to realize our sinful condition, when it would otherwise take a long time for us "good" believers to take off the Pharisee's tunic.

- "They are people like us!" they said of the prisoners when we had finished giving a retreat in the maximum security prison. It struck me that they did not say instead, "We are people like them."

Sinful with all sinners, we may rejoice in God's grace. Entering more deeply into our depth, we are invited to believe and give thanks for God's mercy.

And we begin to be one with all the victims of our societies. It no longer matters whether they are guilty or not; we can see and hear in each of them the desires of a disfigured Jesus. We begin to long and pray for healing, for transfiguration for all. We yearn for the rebuilding of the temples we are, believing in God's promises as told to us by Haggai (2:1-9). Probably too, we want to do our best to bring about a "resurrection" in each one of us, as the Father does. A rehabilitation.

Paradoxically, the knowledge of our "negative" feelings carried by our inner tide invites us further to see beyond appearances. It was the challenge given to the Jews and Gentiles who passed by Golgotha on a Friday afternoon two thousand years ago. They saw a man sentenced to death dying on a cross. Did they hear the cry of his being? Were they amazed to see him, so marred was his appearance? Did they see that "there was no stately bearing to make [them] look at him, no appearance that would attract [them] to him"? Was he "spurned and avoided, a man of suffering"? Did they hide their faces from him, who was "spurned and held in no esteem"? They had to recognize, hear and love the disfigured Son of God, Jesus our Savior.

"POSITIVE" FEELINGS

Thus the way of an initial silence that we do not repress creates within us a passivity and flexibility that allows all the above feelings to come to the surface faster. Therefore the revelations connected with what is happening in our depth may appear to us sooner than would otherwise be the case. This is especially true of the roots of our fears. We might spontaneously think that when the tide of "positive" feelings flows out, our desire might be to swim in it complacently. After all, no one likes to be deaf when he or she hears love songs! But can we be so sure?

• The fact is that many people do not go back to praying the way we have described, even though their first experiences were very good, with an overflow of "positive" feelings. Why this surprising reluctance?

Revelations

Our depth sometimes lets "positive" feelings surface that may seemingly be as powerful as the 'negative" ones. Instead of the usual gentle peace of quiet joy, we know the living water as Ezekiel did in his Temple vision (47:3ff): water flowing ankle-deep, knee-deep, up to our waist and higher still. The strength of the experience, of course, depends on the individual, but it may reach extremes. Invaded by an astounding peace or an explosive joy, overwhelming gratitude or fantastic wonder, we cannot contain it. The body enters painfully into the experience: tears of contrition flow abundantly, we kneel or prostrate ourselves, our heart beats violently, our whole being trembles with delight. Time and space disappear. Though perfectly conscious, we are nowhere. Sometimes our mind holds on to this revelation, and sometimes our heart is enamoured of it for several consecutive days. The world around us has not changed in itself, but it is different for us.

Through these striking reactions or calmer ones, we savor the same feeling of being one with the Lord. Peace and joy point out that a profound "yes" to God exists as a desire within our depths, a "yes" that is sometimes perceived behind our "no's." Our "yes" answers the "yes" said forever by the Father to the son or daughter we are through the Spirit of Jesus.

Sometimes such oneness is felt because we understand how much we have been forgiven. Like the lost son hugged by the Father (Luke 15), or the sinful woman absolved by Jesus (Luke 7), we touch with our fingers the mercy of God. Gratitude fills us. We have been healed: torturing scruples are gone, trying hesitations have disappeared, nagging doubts have vanished. We give thanks for the compassion the Lord has shown us.

Beyond all that, we have always felt ourselves loved. Our faith is reinforced by the "positive" feelings that make more tangible an infinite, absolute, unconditional love. We sometimes wonder, "Do you really love me so much? Really, me?" We give praise.

There grows within us a great desire to give love back in order to be more and more one with the Lord. We desire to love more deeply and faithfully, more constantly and concretely. We are only "yes" with him (2 Corinthians 1: 19). So we say, "I will lay down my life for you!" (John 13:37).

These last words sound familiar to all of us. Because of them, because of Peter, we can understand why some people are reluctant to go back to the powerful experiences that seized them—by praying again, for instance, with the same texts and with the same passivity.

It is not exactly that they want to be deaf or want God to be. The feelings are too good to be refused. (A bit of spiritual greediness is always present.) But they would like to turn down the volume of what they hear in their depth. Why? For the following reasons.

First, we are sometimes frightened by the reactions of our body. Since affectivity is connected with sexuality, we sometimes feel our sexuality awakening through our body. What if it became too strong? We prefer to flee from it. After all, if God heard that, what would he think?

- He needed great courage to remain passive when the Song of Songs became so vivid.

As a matter of fact, I think that behind this fear we are afraid to let all our possible love pour out. We are attracted to saying "yes" through love, but we cannot help withdrawing; for it is a "yes" to what? We are afraid of being called to the foolishness of love that Paul talks about in 1 Corinthians 1. We are too fond of being "wise" persons. We would like to give—but not too fast, not too far, not too much. "I will be your follower, Lord, but first let me take leave of my people." "Let me bury my father first." Two people spoke this way to Jesus (Luke 9:59-60). "But..." God has shown us a treasure, a pearl, in our depth: his own capacity of loving through his Spirit. But we hesitate to sell all we have (Matthew 13:44-45). To love is to risk. Maybe we are like the rich man of the Gospel (Mark 10:21-22).

We would like to escape from what we have heard. We are afraid to be loved too much. If we should by chance be really "seized" (Philippians 3:12), we probably could not resist the attraction of this call. We would be totally "given up," "handed over," saying "Father, thy will be done." Such words sound too much like the Passion of Jesus. If we let a passionate love take control of us, we would rightly reach the point of panic.

Communion with the madness of love

When we can let our depth express these "positive" feelings without resisting too much their powerful call, we enter into communion with all those who have said "yes."

We desire communion with those who silently burned with love, with those whose indelible testimony marks the world and its history. We are one with those who are signs of the Kingdom already among us, with those who have realized Christ's desire when he said, "I have come to light a fire on the earth. How I wish the blaze were ignited!" (Luke 12:49). We hear and become part of the multitude that repeats the words of Jeremiah, "You have seduced me, lord, and I let myself be seduced....I say to myself, I will not mention him, I will speak his name no more. But then it becomes like fire burning in my heart, imprisoned in my bones; I grow weary holding it in, I cannot endure it" (20:7-9).

As passionate lovers we may become one with the martyrs.

Giving our depth the freedom it can take, we discover the "beyond" of our love: a call to go farther and farther. Whether we panic and withdraw, whether we follow our deep desire to serve, we know that a prodigious desire for and power of love dwells within us and urges us to love more tenderly, more faithfully, more concretely.

Someday we can say authentically with the Spirit of Jesus, "Abba!"

It is beyond easy words, the too easy-words of love. We are reminded of Jesus' warning, "None of those who cry out, 'Lord, Lord' will enter the kingdom of God, but only the one who does the will of my Father in heaven" (Matthew 8:21). The call will go on resounding within us if we do not make ourselves deaf. We can hope that tomorrow will see our "yes." No one has the right to judge anyone.

The disciples James and John said "yes," and so did Thomas and Peter. But what had to be accomplished went far beyond what they said, understood and were able to do. We can believe that Jesus' prayer will be for us as it was for Simon: "Simon, I have prayed for you, that your faith may never fail. You in turn must strengthen your brothers" (Luke 22:31-32).

Whether weak or strong, we need Jesus? strength through faith, for love is beyond our power.

SCOBIE

Sometimes what our depth reveals when we are not deaf and when we listen as the Lord does is clear: sometimes nothing, sometimes "negative" feelings, sometimes "positive" feelings. But we can guess from what has already been said that it is not always so simple. We may find ourselves resisting the "negative" feelings or rejecting the attraction of the "positive" ones. So it is not surprising that the tide brings us a mixture. This always reminds me of Graham Greene's *The Heart of the Matter*, whose protagonist, Scobie, loves two women and finally commits suicide. Paradoxically this book, which many consider a masterpiece, in the end suggests that Scobie has never loved anyone but God.

We may see within ourselves, coming to the conscious level, a mixture of desires characterized by great tension and violent struggle. We are torn apart by two equally attractive opposites, both of which may seem equally good. We suffer, because the choice is unclear or painful, or even impossible to make. It is as if a woman were asked to choose between her husband and her children. An impossible choice: so Scobie commits suicide. But the conclusion of the book suggests that the question is too deep to be understood and judged in black and white.

Revelations

It is already difficult to discover that we are "yes" and "no" at the same time, but it is even worse to be unable to make a choice. It is most terrible when we cannot decide between one good "yes" and another.

First of all, we understand that things are not always clear and simple. Human beings are characterized by ambiguity. Here, too, we would like to make God deaf, even though he knows very well the clay of which we are made, and that we are not pure and perfect spirits. But we are not realistic, so ashamed are we to be mixed up. We would so much like to be deaf in order to forget this kind of cry so difficult to deal with.

Then we begin to understand the mystery of the human heart. At a certain level of depth, our being may be torn apart and almost unable to avoid a dead end. Yes, a dead end: a place where we die to self. The experience of "negative" feelings helps us die to the "no" we are; with the "positive" ones we die to the "yes." But we go on living, with the two liberating a priceless "yes." As Scobies, we die…period. We die to the possibility of having and saying the last word. No or yes, yes or no, the last word is simple and gratifying. (Self-satisfaction might have its way!) As Scobies, we no longer know how we may be unified within ourselves. We are only torn.

Communions

No longer do we find in ourselves room to judge hesitant and weak people, the ones we could easily call cowards, because we cannot see their hearts. No longer can we easily advise or judge those who give up and break. For many of them, obedience and fidelity are wished for but impossible. There can be no sarcasm on our lips for those torn apart between two promises, honors or fidelities. There is no easy verdict. We can understand and be one with people who pray for death or decide on suicide. It is strange to see how easily the mystics understand such people.

- How deeply was I driven into myself when he told me, "If anyone finds out that I am a homosexual, I will commit suicide."

- How deep must we go to stand beside this man who deeply loves his wife and children—and alcohol, too? Tortured but weak, he had learned to be dependent on drink as a young child.

We become one with all people who are torn apart, those for whom the indicated way is not easy, those who suffer from being too weak and erratic, with all of us who are neither pure nor heroic. We are a part of the human mass that has neither the courage nor the rashness, the boldness nor the unconsciousness of the strong ones. We are one with all those consoled by the words of

Jesus, "Let the one among you who has no sin be the first to cast a stone at her" (John 8:7).

All of those people we now hear live out in their desires the agony of powerlessness. In great part, however, salvation was effected during the agony in the garden. The Father heard the struggle going on in Jesus' heart in Gethsemane—the desire to live, the desire to love—before his Son said "Yes, Abba." There Christ shared the ordeal of the Scobies we sometimes are. "In the days when he was in the flesh, he offered prayers and supplications with loud cries and tears to God, who was able to save him from death....Son though he was, he learned obedience from what he suffered" (Hebrews 5:7-8). The author of Hebrews minces no words.

When we are not sure that we express the groanings of the Spirit, because what rises within us is more like a deathrattle, it is consoling to say to him, "You know." Indeed, "You know everything. You know well that I love you" (John 21:17).

In this kind of experience we are driven to discover something beyond ourselves, beyond the "me" we usually perceive. A beyond that impels us to go back to the act of faith that opened this book, the faith that sustains our initial silence. "Beyond anything I can grasp about myself, you, Father, hear me, you listen to me, you understand me" Augustine expressed it, *"Intimior intimo meo, superior summo meo."*

> Out of the depths I cry to you, 0 Lord;
> Lord, hear my voice!
> Let your ears be attentive
> to my voice in supplication" (Psalm 130:1-2).

He, our Abba, *knows* our desires. He only.

Our initial silence helps us in our exodus to go beyond the ordinary boundaries of what we know about ourselves, others and God. With all those we can now hear, we cross the Red Sea with only the minimum of baggage, without fear, as one of God's people. We enter into and discover a new land that becomes our own. In communion with others, we desire to conquer the unknown part of ourselves with the Lord's help. His covenant with us assumes a deeper significance, revealing him as close to us and beyond any sign. Each cry unfolds and deepens the mystery of ourselves, others and God.

This will go on until the day we cross our last Red Sea, death, and faith is no longer necessary, when we see "face to face...and know as we are known" (1 Corinthians 13:12) in love. Then we will give forth our last earthly cry and begin the everlasting cry of praise: "Abba."

"WHAT IS YOUR NAME?"
(Exodus 3:13)

We began by establishing that everyone prays everywhere and always because God hears the happy or unhappy cry with which we are pregnant. Then we proposed that we begin our prayer with silence. Sustained by a minimum of necessary signs, this attitude keeps our inner depth from being hidden behind the frequently used masks of formalization. We have examined the revelations and the communions that come to consciousness through such behavior. If we dare to face this initial silence, these revelations and communions come to the surface more quickly as a general rule than they would through the slow process of materializing our prayer. Our fears are removed more quickly, and freedom is given to our deepest feelings.

When our cries are delivered into our consciousness like a tide, a certain formalization takes place; for it is impossible not to express strong and powerful feelings. Then the ordinary process of materialization begins, of which we have summarized the benefit and necessity for us. We become conscious so that we can discern and assume our responsibility in faith and love. But even here the savor of our initial silence will not leave us. We will keep a wholesome distance from spiritual greed and narcissism, from escape and fear. We shall have relished so much the inestimable value of passivity and flexibility; we shall have appreciated so much our growth in faith, that we shall go back to silence with joy and without apprehension. The desire for silence will impel us to go back more quickly to a silent prayer. The Promised Land of the ultimate silence will make itself known without delay. Often we multiply signs because we cannot express a desired "beyond," but now we know that the best way to do so is the way of silence in faith and love.

We emphasize the phrase, "to go back." Indeed what appears in many books to be a "going toward" is in fact a "going back." We go back to being silent with the Lord, to his listening to our heart. He has been listening since the time he knit us in our mother's womb (Psalm 139:13), when he first desired us. Since our beginning he has been listening to our heart...and he knows how much of that time our lips were mute. He was already listening to the cries of our being that were fashioned by our heredity. In his desire he had already chosen us, saying lovingly.

> But now, thus says the Lord,
> who created you...and formed you;
> Fear not, for I have redeemed you;
> I have called you by name: you are mine.

When you pass through the water, I will be with you;
in the rivers you shall not drown.
When you pass through fire, you shall not be burned;
the flames shall not consume you.
For I am the Lord, your God...your Savior...
Because you are precious in my eyes and glorious,
and because I love you.
Fear not, for I am with you (Isaiah 43:1-5).

Yes indeed, we believe that he has always listened to us, as a physician listens to a beating heart, as a lover listens to a heart that loves.

The Lord listens to the "beyond" in us, to that inexpressible depth of self that anticipates and appeals to a silence that was accepted in the beginning and sought after in the end. That inexpressible point of self that we cannot know or pronounce, our deepest name; the person we are beyond anything we may discover. The Father listens unceasingly to our name, because he lovingly desires this echo of his own Son through their Spirit, because it is an echo of his own Name—the name inexpressible for Israel. It is time for us to be still.

COWLEY PUBLICATIONS is a ministry of the Society of St. John the Evangelist, a religious community for men in the Episcopal Church. Emerging from the Society's tradition of prayer, theological reflection, and diversity of mission, the press is centered in the rich heritage of the Anglican Communion.

Cowley Publications seeks to provide books, audio cassettes, and other resources for the ongoing theological exploration and spiritual development of the Episcopal Church and others in the body of Christ. To this end, it is dedicated to developing a new generation of theological writers, encouraging them to produce timely, creative, and stimulating publications of excellence, and making these publications available widely, reaching both clergy and lay persons.